OUR TRAVEL ROUTE LAST SUMMER.

Hell-o! —

The format of this book is kind of choppy and crude — cut and pasted together like a fucked up mosaic with different people's thoughts and stories and pictures and poems and art and flyers interspersed between my own stories and feelings about setting up the Nomadic Festival and traveling around the country last Summer. The whole thing has been a couple months in the works and of course there are a ton of left out details and chapters, a lot of raw, unedited stories thrown together at the last second in a fury cause I'll be damned if I spend another day in front of a fucking computer when I could be outside somewhere having fun.

This project as it stands now was put together between the beginning of September 1995 and the end of January 1996. It was written on five different macintosh compters, an old electric typewriter, and lots of little scribbled napkins and shit.

This book was originally published as a zine. Only 20 copies are floating around. It seemed like too much of a pain in the ass to try and scam a zillion copies so I convinced Mr. Sascha that a bound book would be better and be more durable. —Scott

Bloodlink Press   PO Box 7414   Phila PA 19101
please send sase for catalog of stuff...

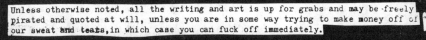

CREATE
THE
WEB

This is the story of our Traveling Outlaw Party. Our Dropout
Circus. Our Carnival of Chaos. The whole sordid tale, from when
we left New York in June, to when we all went our separate ways
in Minneapolis, two and a half months later. It's the story of
one person's ridiculous crackpot idea flowering into a summer of
radical festivals and sometimes very strange gatherings around
the country. It's the story of a bunch of clueless but slightly
talented people, not at all knowing what they were doing, racing
against time along the highways and the train lines, not always
knowing why, but somehow managing to make it across that country
with virtually no money. It's the story of a bunch of very
different networking subcultures. The cultures underground -
feeding off the wastes of a dying parent culture - growing out of
the cracks in the cement like weeds, slowly taking root under all
the strip malls and the jails. It's a story about not being able
to stay in one place or sit still for too long. It's a story
about eating out of the garbage and walking around with
firecrackers in your pockets all the time. This is a story about
Life. Not Life the cereal. Not Life the boardgame. Not Life the
magazine. This is a very real story about very real people in a
very fucked up world, trying to create something different for
themselves and the people around them. It's a story about
breaking down barriers and putting up walls, building bridges and
burning them down. It's a story about riding freight trains
through the mountains with a bunch of good friends. It's a story
about traveling around with a crew of drug-crazed maniacs. It's a
story about walking into the middle of extremely bizarre
situations and walking away from them with your head spinning,
wondering what actually happened. It's a cut and paste story, a
million little pieces of paper glued together in the middle of
the night, a million different untold sides to that same weird,
half-imaginary circus elephant, wandering the streets of some
small town after everybody's asleep. It's a story of wild
ecstatic success and no hope crash and burn failure. Whatever it
is, it's a damn good story - check it out:

INDEPENDENT
SURVIVAL SYSTEMS

Hop on my Late Night Train of Thought for a Second cause it's a Totally Long Scatter Ramble

I'm sitting by my window at four in the morning right now at this very minute and I can hear the buzz of the city - the traffic - the horns wailing angry in the distance - the car alarms squealing their eight part symphonies - the police sirens barking their red and blue orders - I can feel the blaring orange and yellow lights tacked up on every street and the noise of the garbage trucks and street cleaners making their way up the avenues. I'm living smack in the middle of this crazy nightmare of a society and it's spinning out of control, and I can feel it cause I'm sitting in the heart of the beast and I was raised here - it's so much a part of me I can't even tell you: all the blank and hateful stares walking down the street and all the buildings blocking out the sky(there are no stars here), all the puddles of neon green anti-freeze and rainbow oilslick sludge collecting on the edge of the sidewalks and all the hours I've spent biking in traffic and all the cathode ray images burned into my head that I didn't want or I didn't know I didn't want and the enormous subway tunnels we dug into the earth - and that manic time's running out shit and all the fucking noise in my head. I'm a product of my world.

Just listen to how I talk and what I talk about. I didn't hear any crickets chirping outside my window as I was going to sleep as a kid and I didn't hear any birds singing in the morning when I went off to school. And I had it good cause I was raised with a family that told me I could do whatever I wanted when I grew up and so I believe it now and I'm not totally fucked up. But I'm surrounded by lost souls and broken dreams and that cycle of poverty - we're all so far away from our dreams. I'm not sure how we got here but this is the future right now - but it's more than the future because it's the present - and really it's so much a part of me I have no choice but to thrive off it - and I love it because I have to because it's a part of me. But see I'm not stupid and I don't play by the rules, because the rules were obviously written by fools.

TRUST YOUR DESIRES

Everything around me is fueled by mass production and mass consumption and mass stupidity and mass denial and it can't go on like this forever. See, I know that the planners are sitting in their offices planning their plans to carve up our neighborhood - build more luxury condominiums for the rich and more massive housing projects for the poor, kick us out of the squats and keep the cycle going. It's all tied together. I know that rich men in expensive suits sit around big tables in high office buildings right here in this very city and plan the obsolescence of products before they even try and market them to me and everyone else around me. They make things so that they break quickly so that we'll want to buy more of them. And there's more and more shit lining the streets every day. I know that millions of dollars are spent on market research and advertisements every year, trying to figure out ways to convince me and everyone else around me that we need things newer, faster, better, cleaner, bigger, smaller, whatever.

I know that thousands of pounds of edible food are thrown away every day by supermarkets and restaurants in cities all over this country so that we continue to pay retail prices for food.

I know that big companies pollute our water with their chemicals and waste and then other big companies try and sell us purified designer water in plastic bottles with slick market campaigns and there are people out their who actually buy designer water, and I don't understand that.

The government subsidizes gasoline prices so that companies continue to build cars, and people continue to buy cars, and states continue build highways for the cars, and you know that this can't go on forever. None of this can go on forever.

Most people in this world are starving. People in this country starve themselves voluntarily. People in third world countries learn to reuse and recycle everything out of necessity. In this country we have to dig large holes in the ground so we can bury all our trash. Things are very fucked up.

This is how it's perpetuated: there's this work ethic myth in our culture that if you work hard all day and pay your mortgage and pay your taxes and pay your car bills and don't take any handouts - you're an independent person. But the reality is that the last thing any of us are in this world is independent. You go buy a sandwich on your lunch break at your job and think about independence for a minute. There are so many people between you and that sandwich you're eating - from the people who picked the lettuce in the fields, to the people who baked the bread, to the people in the factory farm who raised that genetically engineered mutant chicken, to the people who delivered all the stuff in the trucks, to the guy who put the whole thing together in the back, to the guy who took your money to anyone else who had anything to do with it and all their friends and relatives and everyone they know. It's like that old AT&T commercial: "We're all Connected." There's no such thing as independence. Everything you buy or sell feeds into that whirlwind of capital and affects everyone around you. We are all connected. And I'll tell you something else: it looks to me like money has replaced the role our families played in earlier times. You don't need friends or family if you have a big checkbook and a credit card. We live in little boxes stacked up on top of each other and we're taught that it's in our nature to step on other people to get where we want. The same thing that connects us all is tearing us to pieces.

We're so far away from each other. We're so far away from each other.

Luckily I realize all this and I have lots of crafty and beautiful friends who realize it too. There are a bunch of us out here who are fed up with the current situation and are trying to opt out of this crazy world and create something better for ourselves so that us and our kids and their kids if we ever get that far along, don't have to be surrounded by this culture of waste and death. We even already have the beginning seeds of a plot. But I'll tell you a little secret: as much as we try and create our own culture and rise above the ways we've been raised, slip out of that wage slave rat race mold and fend for ourselves, it's so hard to break out of the cycles we've been taught. There are so few tools to work with or stable foundations - our lives always seem based on instability and transience. We're always finding ourselves back in the same basic struggles with the world around us and with each other.

SURVIVAL

We even use the language of the dominant culture, sometimes so subtle: "We **spent** all that time...It's none of your **business**...I'll **buy** that..." It's like we're programmed consumers. We're tied into the game because we were born into it. We have so much potential but we're all a bunch of junkies and cripples; we're addicted to our conveniences and our pain medicines; we're a mess. This is how things **work**.

But we're learning. Every year, more of us get fed up with our lives and start dropping out - opting out of the no future time clock existence we see all around us. We're experimenting with different living systems and alternative communities, networking our own underground support systems.

We're learning together how to outsmart the system, to live outside the system as outlaws. We're learning more about moving past our differences and working together, pooling our resources and stealing the rest.

The system's fucked - can't you see? There's always going to be a few rich fuckers at the top sucking off of everyone else's life and there's always going to be the poor people slaving away for the rich people. Useless work is shit and it can take the best years of your life if you don't watch out and we're living those years right now and we're not going to waste them.

Some people call us parasites because we tap into the resources of the hyperdeveloped industrial grid and pick the over-ripe fruits off the massproduction tree as we struggle to build our own independent world underground.

6

But who are the real parasites? When you're a parasite it means you live at the expense of others' without making any useful return.

So does that person who owns a string of convenience stores selling overpriced fast food and gas along the highway provide a service to the public? Are the Chief Executive Officers of multi-national corporations who are systematically destroying our planet and raping its people for their own profit actually upstanding citizens? When did our values get turned on our heads?

So like I said, there are a bunch of us who want no part of this shit. We're trying to create independent survival systems for ourselves and looking for people who are fed up like we are and want to build something better for the future. We want to create our own centers of attraction instead of always being pulled to the

marketplace, bring people from everywhere together to create autonomous zones where the government can't touch us, learn from each other and our different triumphs and mistakes and experiences, cut out all the middlemen and corporations, barter and trade through our own networks, keep exchange within our own community, revel in our lives and realize our true potential, emerge from the waste like the phoenix in that old beautiful myth.

We don't have any capital behind us or slick ad campaigns. We steal from big companies and write graffiti and broadcast our words of protest on pirate radio and in little zines like this - but we have soul. And I'll tell you right now that there is a difference between being poor in pocket and poor in soul. And that's what this story is all about.

NOMAD CULT

JANUARY 26th, 1996
THE SUN IS RISING.

I WISH I WAS A PIGEON IN THE SKY.

THE BEGINNING:

THIS ALL STARTED FOR ME LAST JANUARY. I WAS HANGING OUT ONE COLD AFTERNOON IN 7TH STREET SQUAT WITH ARROW, STEPHANIE, PASTRAMI, AND FLY. ARROW WAS SHOWING US THE ROUGH DRAFT OF A LETTER HE WAS ABOUT TO SEND OUT TO A BUNCH OF PEOPLE ALL OVER THE COUNTRY, THE BEGINNING SEEDS OF A PLOT HE HAD TO ORGANIZE A BAND OF ANARCHISTS AND ARTISTS AND FREAKS TO TRAVEL AROUND IN THE SUMMERTIME AND HAVE WEEK LONG FESTIVALS AND WORKSHOPS WHERE EVER THE CLIMATE SEEMED RIGHT TO DO IT. WE HAD TALKED ABOUT IT A BIT BEFORE AND MY MIND WAS SWIMMING WITH IDEAS OF GUERILLA THEATER PRANKS AND STORIES I HAD HEARD ABOUT THE TRAVELERS MOVEMENT IN EUROPE - THOUSANDS OF PEOPLE MOVING FROM TOWN TO TOWN, OLD GYPSY STYLE, CREATING FESTIVALS AND DISRUPTING LOCAL ECONOMIES. I THOUGHT ABOUT ALL THE AMAZING AND TALENTED PEOPLE ON THE ROAD AND WHAT IT WOULD BE LIKE TRAVELING WITH A BIG PACK OF PEOPLE, CARAVANING ON THE HIGHWAY AND SHOWING UP IN TOWNS WITH A WHOLE BUNCH OF SUPPLIES AND INSPIRATION, PUTTING ON PERFORMANCES AND SPREADING INFORMATION ABOUT DIFFERENT POLITICAL MOVEMENTS AND CHECKING OUT RADICAL SCENES AROUND THE COUNTRY AND FINALLY CONVINCING PEOPLE TO DROP OUT AND COME WITH US. I LEFT NEW YORK A COUPLE DAYS LATER AND TREKED AROUND THE COUNTRY FOR THREE MONTHS, GIVING FLYERS TO COOL PEOPLE I MET ALONG THE WAY. ANYWAY, WE'RE BACK AT 7TH STREET AND IT'S THE MIDDLE OF WINTER. I REMEMBER WE WERE SITTING AROUND TALKING AND ARROW WAS PASSING AROUND THIS FRESHLY PRINTED PAPER, ALL PROUD AND EXCITED, AND PASTRAMI READS OUT SOME TYPO OR GRAMMER FUCKUP IN THE FIRST LINE AND SAYS IN HIS THICK BROOKLYN ACCENT AND TWINKLING DARK EYES: "OH GREAT. FOLLOW ME - I'M STUPID!" AND WE WERE ALL CRACKING UP. SO, FOR WHAT IT'S WORTH, THAT WAS MY FIRST MEMORY OF THE NOMADIC FESTIVAL.

NOMADIC FESTIVAL '95

Hello. My name is Arrow. I'm an Anarchist-Squatter on the Lower East Side of New York City. I'm sending you this letter because I got a great idea for a party this summer. Lets call it a Nomadic Festival.

I've been traveling around the country every summer for the past four years, train-hopping or hitch-hiking, visiting warehouses and squats in the cities and farms and intentional communities in the rural areas, going to punk-fests, anarchist gatherings and even a rainbow gathering. I find that traveling with little or no money is usually a great way to go cuz you meet lot's of people and are forced to use creative means to survive. Being at home with the television and newspapers can sometimes be such a depressing reminder of what a stifling repressive , close-minded, money-grubbingly capitalistic, decadent, apathetic, conservative and un-creative country we live in. But, I'm always amazed at how many truly radical, creative, inspiring people I meet when I'm out there on the road. And they're just as fed up with Americas bullshit as I am. I mean there are so many little anarchist communities, hyper-active punk bands, radical ecologist, awe-inspiring performance troops, rugged survivalists, mad-genius poets, hyper-media activists, super-heal er herbalists and just plain freedom fighters of all shapes and sizes creating their own little piece of a new society right here, and now, but the problem is ... isolation. I mean, you can't read about this stuff in the morning news over cheerios. You got to get out there, you got to find it. The problem with isolation is, it keeps us from inspiring each other and from being able to build on what others have done.

So, what I think we need to do is get out there, meet, and interact without any T.V. screens or papers to hide behind and manipulate our reactions. Break down the walls of isolation and party our asses off. And create. A network. A nomadic festival. An anarchist circus. An outlaw party. An autonomous educational exchange. An anti-capitalist orgy. A symphony of souls.

So I've spoken with a lot of people about this nomadic festival and the shape of it seams to be this: It will be a 3 month journey around the U.S. We'll figure out about 13 locations. We'll spend approximately one week in each spot. We'll spend this week taking over abandoned housing, procuring mass quantities of free food and supplies, indulging in various forms of cultural and poetic terrorism, and building for the 'event', which will take place on the weekend. 'The event' could be workshops and info exchange in the day and an open-mic-style party at night, and then more workshops or activities the next day and a big party with live music and dancing and art that night. And then sunday comes and we shake off our hangovers, say our goodbye's, and head out to the next location. Hopefully with a bunch of new friends from the party. Will we have dine and dash food fights in the most expensive restaurant in town? Will we have an orgy on the steps of the capital? Will we blow up the local police precinct? Will we plant trees in cars in the business district? The possibilities are endless but everything depends on the flavor of the traveling group and the local spice of the area.

I thought we could begin to form an itinerary by the responses I get from this letter. The basic plan is to leave new york in early june and head south. Then make our way zig-zagging west. Spiraling up the west coast. Then swaying and swaggering back east. I'm hoping that we'll have local people in every location anticipating our arrival and helping to hook us up when we get there. Also to let other locals know we're coming.

NOMADIC FESTIVAL

I really need your input here because this nomadic festival should be created and organized by everyone involved in it, not just a handful. No one will be in charge, and hopefully everyone will take charge. So if you're interested please send your opinions on. Would you like to participate as a traveler? Would you like to host an event in your area? Do you think one week is too long or too short for each location? Some people would like to forget the idea of having an itinerary altogether, although I think it's necessary so that people will know when to expect us and so that people may 'jump on the train' once it is moving. What do you think? What sort of performances should we have? Workshops? Some ideas and themes I'd like to include are: solar power, alternative home-building, herbology, home-made drugs, scams (of all sorts), midwifery, home-schooling, squatting, sustainable agriculture, media pranks and culture jamming, pirate radio/T.V., sensuality art, body art, music, poetry, dancing, etc., etc.

I'm hoping that the nomadic festival will be very radical and very creative. I'd like to keep the events free and open to anyone to encourage an anti-capitalist atmosphere. I hope that through bartering and gift giving we can create real alternatives to this death cult capitalist nightmare we call AMERICA and begin to build independent survival systems for our cultures, as the old systems of 'too late' capitalism collapse around us.

I will be sending this letter to anyone who I think will be interested in participating in the Nomadic Festival. Obviously ther are probably a lot of folks who would love to be involved that I don't know. So please, if you know anybody who might be in to it, give 'em a copy of this letter. And remember to write back! I will compile all the responses and put them out in a little 'zine-letter around the end of March. If you want to go on the whole journey plan on being in New York June 1st for the Take-Off party. Oh, almost forgot, it looks like we're gonna have a bus with cooking facilities for the trip so all we need now is: a good PA system; a generator; gallons and gallons of paint; more musical instruments; radio-shack 33# Auto-Dialers; costume supplies; solar-powered vehicals; big pots and pans; shoes; food; money; walkie-talkies; lingerie; drugs; kandie bars; precious metals; cool herbs; computer systems; contained living bacteria; alcohol or anything else you might have lying around that you're just dying to donate to our fantastic journey. Oh, also it would be nice if people sent a couple of stamps with your letter so that I could send you the next issue of the Nom.Fest.Zine.Letter. I guess thats a start....

Arrow ---->

209 EAST 7TH STREET
NEW YORK, NY 10009
212/ 614-0393

A Carnival of Chaos

[illegible]! Welcolm to the Nomadic Festial Organization Newsletter #2. As our informal information [illegible] weaves itself together, and new connections are made we felt it was time to update the mailing. As you can see, the basic itinerary is pretty much the same. We added a bunch of places we'll be passing through to give people an idea of the routes we're taking in hopes of rest spot offers and hooking up with friends. With a bunch of veichles caravaning around, there are bound to be a number of places we'll stopping for gas, doing a little cultural sightseeing at a few malls, maybe a couple makeshift parades on mainstreets in towns. With a number of offers from people to camp on their land in between cities, the shape of our summer trek appears to be taking the form of pulling off big week long parties in the middle of urbanhell and then running off to the woods and desert to relax and play and plan future actions. Becausy it seems as if a lot of folks are going to be meeting up with us along the way we've set up two contact numbers that can be called all summer for current information and locations. Here's the plan:

May 31-June 1: Costume making, silkscreening, and supply gathering parties at Bullet Space

June 2-3:NYC: Two-day long Lower East Side festival/gathering of the souls thang. Friday: La Plaza Cultural and Dos Blocos. Saturday: Bullet Space BBQ and dance party.

June 4-10:Philadelphia: Solar-powered campsite/info-base next to the a space, two warehouse spaces for performances, and a Festival of Popular Delusions street parade. Folks interested in helping to organize this stop call Kristen at (215)-474-6459 or the Wooden Shoe at (215)569-2477.

June 11-17:Ohio-Dayton and elsewhere: Stopping on some land near Buffalo for tune-ups and fresh air, a sleepover at the Anarchist Catholic Worker in Pittsburg, maybe stopping in Columbus and finishing up the week in Dayton. People interested in organizing in Dayton call Jeff at (513)278-7024.

June 18-24:Atlanta: The submarine caravan may be surfacing momentarily in Lexington, Knoxville, and Chattanooga, then dancing with the snakes in Atlanta. A critcal-mass celebration of Aimless Wandering Day (June 21), Food Not Bombs, and a midsummer's eve Festival of Contagious Magic featuring the fantastic dance of Natabari. Those interested call Tonya at The Compound (404)681-5136

June 25-July 1:Arkansas-Eurica Springs and Fayetteville area: Check ffor signs of life in Memphis, slapshot clown act dedicated to the pres. in Little Rock, then some R&R in the beautiful mountains of north-western Arkansas. Some wonderful folks near Eurica have offered there ranch for lodging and support. This will be a nature stop. Arkansas folk interested call or write Nom. Fest. headquarters.

July 2-8:Austin TX: Nomads disappear completely then reappear in Austin. Convergence at The Church for the feast of wilderness lost and wildness gained, the usual plethora of activites, culminating in to the Firecracker Festival of the Raging Bull street circus. Call Balaam at The Church(formally the Chaos Collective) (512)385-5493

July 9-15:The SouthWest As it stands now, we have an entire open week to explore in the desert, be carried by the hands of fate, and make our way to the Bay Area. We probably won't head too far South considering it will be very hot. Wanna' hook up? Call Nom. Fest. H.Q.

July 16-23:Bay Area: The Born of Fire Gathering/Nomadic Fest Convergence. There's a ton of exciting stuff going on. Five days of fun and chaos, for more details or to get involved call Matty at (510)601-7476.

July 23-Aug. 9(at the latest); Secret farm-land/intentional community tour-de-force leading into Eugene, leading into Portland, more farm-fun, leading into Seattle. (Leading to total insanity!)

Aug 6-12:Vancouver BC: We will be doing an abandon warehouse raffle, performances in LaQuina, and an outdoor park ffestival commemorating the birth of Emiliano Zapata. Martha and the La Quena hommies hookin it all up so get involved; (604) 231-6626.

Aug 13-19:Minneapolis MN: The longest haul of the trip! Possible Nom. Fest. sighhtings anywhere in Montana and N. Dakota. In MLPS we'll have coal factory pyrotecnics, puppet theater, apple bobbing in the Mississippi, and the Festival of the Volcano street theatre extraviganza. Interested parties call Steve at (612)222-7911.

Aug 20-26:Dreamtime Village WI: Spawning grounds of inspiration and beauty of all flavors. Defiantly another nature stop.

Aug 27-Sept 2:Chicago IL: The last stop of phase 1, coniciding with a yet un-nammed local freak fair in a huge warehouse! Chicago folks interested call Rich at (312)581-3480.

So there it is, 3 months of total chaos on the down low tip!

We know that life is unprdictable and schedules are made to be changed, so if you would like to meet up with us on the road but can't find us here's a couple of numbers to call; Stefane and Dave-(212) 614-0393 or Matty-(510) 253-5687. We will try to check in with people at these numbers 2 or 3 times a week.

One of the questions I've heard people ask concerning the nom.fest. is this "Sounds great but do you think he can pull it off?" Well the answer to that is defiantly no. Something like this takes way to much organizing for any one person to 'pull off'. The only way the Nom. Fest. will happen is if people can come together and organize it in each location. So it's really up to every one involved weather or not WE can pull it off. And judging from the responses I've gotten so far I feel very confident that we can 'pull it off'.

What I'm hoping is that people in each location can get together and form a little collective that could take care of things like:

1. Getting a space (either inside or out) that we could use for our performances. Preferably somewhere that we can keep our equipment dry, that isn't to succeptable to fire(as fire dancing will undoubtably be part of the performance), and can house 100 people

without getting busted.

2. Getting together a list of good dumpsters, free food distributors, gardens, foraging areas, and soup kitchens that we could hit up for goodies while we're in town.

3. Figuring out where we might be able to crash. This could include camping areas, squattable buildings, living room floors, or whatever.

4. Promoting the event and contacting local performers, artists, and bands that might want to get involved.

In preparing for our arrival people should keep in mind that the idea of this event is to create radical, anti-capitalist, multicultural, sustainable networks to help our peoples free themselves from our repressive society. Keeping each event free and open is the ideal we should work towards. Although the reality of this is that there may not be anyplace in a whole city that can offer space for free, so it might be better to charge a little at the door and have a really good event than to do it for free somewhere that is open to police attack. These sorts of decisions will have to be made by the local organizers. Also it might be a good idea to use positive, pro-active graphics and language in promo stuff so as not to alienate prospective allies. (For instance; a multicultural group of people planting a garden in a smashed up police car as opposed to a punk-rocker smashing a cop car.) Again this type of thing will be up to the organizers. And don't get me wrong and think I am anti-punk or anti-hippy or against any specific sub-culture, I just feel that it's important to include as many of our north american rebels as possible. I feel it's very important to seek out artists and performers from the radical black, latino, and native cultures as well as strong women.

People who're interested in going along with the festival should have a good idea of what there going to do. Bands and performance groups should make sure they can be versatile and adaptable as situations change. If there are people who want to come along but don't really do any kind of art or performance then maybe they'd like to take on other tasks such as food gathering/preparation or working the information tables. People wanting to do workshops should keep in mind that the Nom. Fest. will be action oriented and plan there workshops accordingly. (For instance; Instead of doing a workshop on herbology one might want to organize herb foraging and tincture making.) On the other hand certain topics might not be so easy to actualize (for instance; natural child birth) so if your workshop falls into this type of category don't be discouraged and come along anyway, prepared to organize and facilitate your workshop in a spontaneous manner. Anyone who would like to join our caravan is welcome and should write or call beforehand and let me know the specifics of;

1. What you want to do.
2. Where you want to do it.
3. What you need to do it.
4. And how many people you'll be doing it with.

We will have a band or two coming along but i don't think we want to focus on bands for fear of becoming just another music fest. If it turns out that there are a lot of local bands interested in playing at the event when were in town then maybe it might make sense to do two nights. The question then is should it be one night of music and the other an open mic type performance, or should we mix them up each night? There will be very little to no room in the vehicals coming along so people coming will have to either get a car or be prepared to train hop or hitch-hike. We do have a highly experienced young hobo who will be doing the whole route by freight train and has offered to take others if necessary. And because gas will probably be one of the biggest expenses and grossest materials by the Nom. Fest. I'd kinda' like to encourage folks not to take cars. People should bring camping supplies as we will undoubtably be camping in beautiful nature spots along the way. People should bring money for themselves or have a healthy attitude about being broke as it is quite possible that we won't make any money at our performances. I feel like it's quite important for us to do this whole festival with very little money because we probably won't have any, and, if nothing else to prove that it's possible. O.K. I guess that's about it for now........

PROLOGUE FROM THE LOWER EAST SIDE

I got back to New York at the beginning of May. That whole month before we left is a blurred memory of putting together the zine, sending out mass newsletters, making calls to all these people all over the country I didn't know and lots of people I knew, and a couple I remembered I knew half-way through our conversation, doing late-night Kinko's runs with Arrow, staying up all night and plotting our course with the maps and lists of addresses and calendar spread all over the table (passing out in Arrow and Stephanie's kitchen as the sun was rising), having planning meetings which always seemed to turn into guerrilla theater brain storming sessions and story-telling at Blackout Books, gathering strange theater supplies and leaving them in big piles at Bullet Space, silkscreening little pieces of canvas and selling them for a buck on St. Marks Place or in Tompkins Square.

I set up camp on the roof of Martine and Peter's apartment building (they lived right above a Country Western bar that blasted music till 5:00 AM) and set up my makeshift office every night in the phone booth of Odessa Coffee Shop on Avenue A where I'd usually talk on the phone until they closed and then go up on the roof and scribble furiously in my journal or go wander the streets aimlessly.

It twas exciting times. Arrow had gotten a big pile of responses from the original letter he had sent out and had put together a rough itinerary of places to stop with the caravan.

NOMADIC FESTIVAL
MEETING
OF THE MINDS

DANCERS, ARTISTS, JUGGLERS, POETS, PERFORMERS, MUSICIANS, BANDS, GARDENERS, HERBALISTS, TRIBALISTS, POLITICAL + AND CULTURAL ORGANIZERS GET INVOLVED → WE'RE BUILDING FOR A 2 DAY RADICAL FESTIVAL IN THE LOWER-EAST-SIDE AND THEN TAKING IT AROUND THE COUNTRY! ANYONE WITH IDEAS, ABILITIES, OR INTERESTS SHOULD ATTEND THIS MEETING!
NOMADIC FESTIVAL NYC - JUNE 2 + 3
NOMADIC FESTIVAL USA - JUNE THRU AUGUST

BLACKOUT BOOKS
(50 AVE B BETWEEN 3rd + 4th)
MAY 17th / - 7 PM - 1995

Using people's suggestions and common sense, he'd worked out a route that was a full circle around the entire country and we were doing a pretty good job of getting the word out through the circuit.

We thought everything was running pretty smoothly. Arrow was doing a lot of work on this van Amanda gave him (Red Thunder), on the condition he rescue it from a gas station in Connecticut where it was slowly dying. Pete and Martine went to Ontario to gather some money and supplies before we left. Stacey the badass tribal artist and Ryan the local crazy bike mechanic drunk decided to join our voyage and get out of Fifth street Squat for the summer. This punk guy

---

Danny showed up from Louisiana with a P.A. (whose parents thought the Nomadic Festival was a satanic cult but that's a different story entirely...) This artist woman Diana from Tennessee showed up to travel with us. Our crew was slowly taking shape, there were people organizing stuff all around the country, and we had our two day New York take off party set and ready to go. There was this collective vision a bunch of us had. ■■■ I could feel it taking shape like a whirlwind of energy, everyone's separate ideas bouncing off each other and molding the whole mess into something new every day. I was right in the center of it all, crazed but in my element, helping to orchestrate this abstract chaotic circus thing using everyone's resources and talents, introducing people and watching them explode beautifully off each other, itching to leave town so our vision could become reality.

Then the shit hit the fan and knocked the fucking thing out the window. There was a benefit show at ABC-NO-RIO for the Nomadic Festival two Friday's before we left and I caught a ride from there with Megan and the 2.5 Children crew to Philadelphia to hang out for the weekend and go to the Punkfest. When I left that night everything was cool. I got back that Sunday night and the neighborhood was a warzone.

Our people had been tipped off that the Department of Housing, Preservation, and Development was going to attempt an eviction of three buildings on East 13th Street that had been squatted for more than ten years and that they were moving in with police early in the morning.

UPDATED NOMADIC FESTIVAL WANTS LIST
SUPER- NOMADUPDATE ALLS21

THE SUPER-NOMADIC FESTIVAL WANTS LIST

We've had really good luck getting supplies we've needed donated to get this carnival of mayhem on the road. As this list is being typed, one of our vans donated to the cause by Amanda, is being tuned up and ready to make a test run to Dayton. We got a generator donated to us by Mike in Phili, and a P.A. system is being delivered with it's owner, by Brendan and Diana at this very moment straight from Louisiana. Here's a list of stuff we still need/want to bring on our journey and unleash in your town or stuff we can use while we're visiting. The stuff with one of these (*) things next to it is very important and items with of these (**) things next to it is stuff we need before we leave New York on June 4. If you're organizing things in your place of residence, pass this list around and try and find a good spot where people can bring donated supplies.

**Propane Stove/Canisters of Propane
*A few large Pots and Pans/Storage Containers
Large Water Containers
Food Donations - vegetables, beans, lentils, rice, millet, spelt - we're not picky
Mass quantities of spices would be great
Dog Food
A couple large tarps to set up makeshift tents
**CB Radio's - so we can keep in touch on the road
*Mechanic Connections
Good Walkie-Talkie's
Police Scanner
Reflective Tape to mark cars so we don't lose each other while we're caravaning on the highway
*Bike Racks
Bikes
Mass Amounts of Paint: Spraypaint/Housepaint/Paintbombs
Rollers and Poles
Fire Extinguishers(full or empty(to fill with the liquid of your choice))
*An extentable aluminium ladder (it WE"OWER.)
*Photocopy connections
*Stickerpaper and Stickermaking connections
V.C.R.
*Folding Tables
Good flyers/pamphlets/books to distribute
Stencils
Buckets
Waterbased Silkscreen Ink
Fabric (for costume making and large pieces for banners)
Sewing Machine
Musical Instruments
Fireworks and Firecrackers
Stamps and Ink Pads
*Three Thousand Superballs
Glowsticks
Strobe Light
*Large Parachute
Lots of Bubble Making Stuff
Smoke Machine
Slide Projector
Whiffle Balls and Bats

RESISTANCE MAY BE EXPECTED

Air Horns
Crazy Glue
Squirt Guns
Bull Horns
Pink Flamingo Lawn Ornaments
and Plastic Bugs
Eight Tons of Tofu
Large Bundles of Cash
Your Soul in a Jar
Hell in a Handbasket

The squats on the Lower East Side have a crazy history, starting in the early 1970's when the city was going through a serious economic crisis and landlords, rather than trying to maintain their buildings and collect rent, made it a practice to torch their buildings in order to collect insurance money. Buildings

went up in flames all over the city, leaving many people homeless and by the mid 70's, the Lower East Side was a the neighborhood lined with housing projects and burned out tenement buildings, the same buildings that had housed European immigrants at the turn of the century and Latino immigrants a few decades later. Heroin was the main economy of the whole area and no one with money wanted to live anywhere in the general vicinity. But the neighborhood has always had a rich tradition of radicalism and underground artists, from the turn of the century when European immigrants were bringing over the new foreign ideas of anarchism and socialism, to the 50's and 60's when the Tompkins Square Park and Alphabet City became the main stamping grounds for the beatniks and hippies in New York.

When people from the neighborhood started breaking into the condemned buildings in the late 70's, kicking out the junkies who used them as shooting galleries and fixing them up with a vision of homesteading the empty shells and creating a new life for themselves, the city at first tried to stop it with plans of controlled sweat equity programs, and then when those programs failed, virtually ignored it.

Over the next ten years, more and more of the buildings were taken over by groups of urban squatters, trying to forge autonomous lives for themselves and escape the vicious slave cycles of work and rent, putting their sweat and money into the buildings rather than working and paying rent to people they didn't know. Squatter collectives and community gardens sprang up all over the place, filling up the empty buildings and vacant lots of a once seemingly destroyed neighborhood.

Unbeknownst to the city, there was a thriving subculture rising up out of the charred rubble. Bypassing the whole economic arrangement of labor in exchange for wages, the squatters had created a strong work ethic based on direct physical labor - renovating their individual spaces and the overall structure of their buildings with scavenged supplies, water and electricity tapped from the city's underground channels, and help from each other.

A totally unorthodox housing movement that challenged the whole basis of private property rights, the squatters were a strange patchwork group of people: from Latino families who were raised in the neighborhood, to poor artist groups who couldn't afford the escalating rents over in SOHO, to anarchist revolutionaries who wanted to see the whole capitalist system crumble. A flourishing alternative community with connections to other communitites like it around the world, the squats on the Lower East Side became an example to radical groups in other cities of how to create free housing. There was always a lot going on and people passing through town.

Every summer, all these traveler kids would show up from all over the country to hang out and take over one or two buildings to use as crash pads. While most of them would be gone come the end of August, there was always one new building of dedicated workers, busy repairing and insulating their new home before Winter hit, learning the ropes from the older squatters who had been around for a while.

By the late 80's, the city was starting to wise up to the potential the squatters movement had for real social change and the real estate developers started realizing the potential of the newly improved neighborhood for profit. A wave of squat evictions began and condominiums and hip cafes started creeping down along the avenues. The massive riots between the squatters and the police in Tompkins Square Park, which began in 1988 and ended in 1991 when the park was closed down for "renovation", were signals of a new era for the neighborhood. The last four years have seen the rise of massive gentrification and a push to get anyone without money out of the Lower East Side. That's about where we are today, stuck trying to build a stable community in a neighborhood that's quickly changing into yuppie hell.

The five buildings on 13th Street had been in the middle of a losing court battle with the city for almost a year and had become a symbol to many squatters of the new hardships that were waiting in the future under the Guiliani administration.

When I showed up from Philadelphia that night, people had been in the street for hours building barricades and preparing for a police battle, talking nervously in the street and hoping that the squatter lawyers could get an injunction before the raid took place.

NEW YORK, WEDNESDAY, MAY 31, 1995

Before they were evicted, squatters on East 13th Street in Manhattan taunted police officers in riot ge Thirty-one people were arrested as the police emptied two buildings, but there were no serious injuries

People who never seemed to be around had come out of the woodwork to support the buildings and there was food being served and music blasting out of one of the buildings. The cops were slowly starting to gather on both sides of the block and people were welding the doors shut and forming human barriers. By the morning the whole circus of media was there with camera crews and guys with suits and microphones giving live reports. Finally, at about 10am, when there were only about 80 of us in the street and in the buildings, the city unleashed its forces in full glory. Three hundred police in full riot gear, three police helicopters flying really low and swarming around, a swat-team with

Riot Police Remove 31 Squatters From Two East Village Building

By SHAWN G. KENNEDY

With a show of force befitting a small invasion, the Police Department seized two East Village tenements yesterday, overwhelming a defiant group of squatters who had resisted city efforts to retake the buildings for nearly nine months.

Using a tanklike armored vehicle and carrying riot gear, the officers moved in on the city-owned buildings to try to end years of occupation by the squatters, who have argued that their long-term presence and efforts to rehabilitate the once-abandoned buildings gave them the right to stay.

The takeover of the two buildings at 541 and 545 East 13th Street came about mid-morning yesterday, many hours after the police first arrived and were met by makeshift barricades consisting of old furniture, appliances and trash containers.

Well before dawn, the block between Avenue A and Avenue B was filled with dozens of squatters and their sympathizers who danced,

clash between the police and r dents occurred in the summer 1988.

And although the police had pected a violent conclusion to eviction process, in the end mos the squatters yielded peacefully police arrested 31 people, mos whom tried to form a human chai front of the building, there were serious injuries.

The show of force was ordered city officials, in an effort to ins the safety of Buildings Departm workers who actually carried out evictions. Although the city has months been seeking a court d sion that would give them the r to retake five buildings on the bl officials won a more judicial limit ruling last week saying they c evict people from the two buildu because inspectors felt they wer danger of collapse.

At a news conference in the al noon, Mayor Rudolph W. Guil

14

Mac-10 assault rifles, snipers and cops with video cameras on all the roofs next to the buildings, and finally a huge blue and white tank rolling down the street. They finally arrested everyone in the street and pulled everyone else out of the buildings. It was insanity and it was a mess and everyone was scared they were coming for their building next.

The next few days were surreal. It was a lot of angry, sleep deprived squatters freaking out around the neighborhood. It was going to court en Masse and watching Stanley Cohen, squatter lawyer hero, verbally whip the city lawyer's ass. It was really large, inspiring, eviction watch meetings. It was the police showing their presence in the neighborhood more than they ever had and pissing everyone off. It was a lot of things.

Meanwhile, back to the festival, we're supposed to leave in a couple days but all of a sudden we don't have our shit together at all. The day we're supposed to have our costume making party none of us show up. Everyone's so frazzled from the past week it seems impossible that we'll get our shit together to leave. It's hard to be festive with the threat of eviction looming over your head. That Friday we set up the PA and the generator at La Plaza and some people hung out and there was a show at Dos Blockos across the street, but the energy was really tense. Some random person went around and dosed a lot of people with acid so there are probably quite a few different stories about that night then the one I'm telling.

The next afternoon at Bullet Space was a mad house. People started gathering around 1:00PM to make costumes and set up for the party that night. The plan was to have a parade around the neighborhood and then meet up later but I couldn't imagine how it was all gonna come together so quickly. But slowly, more and more people started showing up and hanging out in the street. These guys from Austin, on their way to Europe to go tour around with Crash Worship, brought these huge amazing puppet heads they had created and were lending them out. Everyone seemed to be putting on masks or painting their faces. Then Rolando and a bunch of other people built a cardboard tank out of boxes and tin strips and painted it blue and white, mocking the city's ridiculous show of force only a couple days earlier. All of a sudden, with the help of a few instigators, there was a parade in full swing with a hundred people marching down Avenue C chanting "No Housing No Peace" and dancing around with this huge cardboard tank.

15

NOMADIC FESTIVAL

A FORTNIGHT OF DAYS

Booted squatters, cops clash 2d time

By MICHAEL E.S. CLAFFY and MICHAEL G. ALLEN
Daily News Staff Writers

Squatters evicted from three lower East Side buildings this week marched back to reclaim their squalid homes yesterday — and immediately clashed with baton-wielding cops who forcefully dispersed them.

Five protesters were arrested and charged with rioting. Two Manhattan South Tank Force officers were injured by flying rocks and bottles.

Afterward, the squatters and their supporters retired to a spot near Tompkins Square Park and ranted against the Mayor Giuliani, Police Commissioner William Bratton and "the scum-sucking media."

Deputy Police Inspector Richard Graf and about 200 protesters appeared on E. 13th St. at around 2:30 p.m. and attacked 20 officers standing guard at Nos. 539, 541 and 545.

At those buildings last Tuesday, 200 officers had moved in to forcibly evict the squatters who had for nine months frustrated the city's efforts to dislodge them to make way for new low-income housing.

Thirty-one squatters were arrested at that time as police helicopters circled overhead and Bratton ordered in "Any Time Baby," the NYPD's 30,000-pound armored personnel carrier, to smash through barricades put up by the decrepit buildings' illegal residents.

"I feel really angry that they came in and brutalized people," said Mandy Grape, a 21-year-old CUNY student who marched in the protest and said she was Maced by cops.

"I'm angry that people lost their homes," she said. "They put their entire lives into building up those homes."

"Before [the squatters]

came here," agreed another marcher, who identified herself only as Janet, "they had shooting galleries in there. There were junkies and various other criminals in there. When the squatters took it

over, they cleaned it up."

Last night's marchers carried on the scene with crude cardboard-and-plywood replicas of the police tank that had routed the squatters last week. Police confiscated it

---

It was like no demonstration I've ever seen. Everyone was decked out in these crazy costumes like it was a circus. Keith and Stephanie were blowing these immence fireballs in the air. There were puppets and banners and fake money being thrown all over the place and set on fire. There were children running around with painted faces and people in wheelchairs holding signs. It was beautiful. The momentum was picking up and it became pretty clear we were headed toward 13th Street. As we rolled around the corner with our tank and our firecrackers and shit, all these funny looking people dressed up for a parade started turning over the barricades and totally scaring the

hell out of the cops on duty who quickly brought in mass reinforcements. So we're making all this noise, knocking stuff over, yelling and screaming, and then suddenly a ton of cops show up, destroy our tank, mace everyone in the crowd, and arrest a whole bunch of people. Everyone fled the scene and headed to Tompkins Square Park, where

a bunch of people actually made very moving spontaneous speeches and then the crowd dispersed. Thus ended the first Nomadic Festival Street Parade, New York style..

SQUATTER TANK ROLLS OVER SQUAT KOPS!!
By Chris Flash

Cops were again caught with their pants down as activists raided their positions in a hit and run raid on June 3.

Four days after the eviction of squats on 13th Street by riot cops, machine gun toting SWAT teams and an armored tank for visual intimidation, the anarchist and squatter community decided to respond with a raid of their own, complete with a home-made tank.

Days earlier, with participation from the annual Nationwide Nomadic Festival, activists created banners, masks, wild outfits and a prop tank named "Little Rudy." (In honor of the mayor), made of cardboard.

On June 3 at 8:00 pm, a parade of more than 100 people made their way up the police line barriers in front of 539 and 541 East 13th. Cops on the street were caught almost completely by surprise by the marchers' arrival as roof tops ran down

At the party that night at Bullet I was sleeping in the printshop and having these crazy dreams about cops and carnivals and the desert sky, so get someone else to tell you about it if you want the details. We spent Sunday and Monday packing the vans - Black Box and Red Thunder. We piled a ton of stuff into those vans: a PA, a generator, stacks of zines, two boxes of books from Autonomedia, two trunks full of costumes and props, tools, silkscreens, paint, food, everyone's packs, Blue Dog (our fearless leader). It was a fleeing of the city as much as it was the beinning of a nomadic trek. Nine of us left for Philadelphia that Monday evening, characteristically late and messy, happy to be out of the war zone and wondering what strange things the future was waiting to unleash upon us.

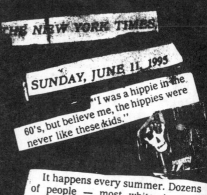

THE NEW YORK TIMES

SUNDAY, JUNE 11, 1995

"I was a hippie in the 60's, but believe me, the hippies were never like these kids."

It happens every summer. Dozens of people — most white, in their teens and 20's — with spiked and rainbow-colored hair and lip and eyebrow rings descend on the Lower East Side from Florida, California, Georgia, Louisiana, Colorado and Oregon. They call themselves nomads and anarchists; others call them "crusties" or "gutter punks" because their clothes are tattered and filthy.

This year, estimates of the itinerant anarchists ranged up to 300, with many arriving last Saturday. Some were responding to a message that was posted on the Internet identifying the lot as the site of a "Nomadic Festival." !!?!

DA' CREW RYGHT BEFORE WE LEFT

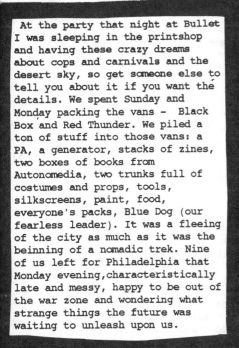

THE PHILADELPHIA EXPERIMENT

A couple days before we all showed up as a group, me and Pete drove down to Philadelphia to pick up the generator from Mike Stalag 13 and talk to a couple of the West Philly anarchist folks about the festival. Making the phone rounds beforehand, I discovered a couple things about the scene there. One: all the anarchist squats, houses, bookstores, and cafes seemed to have voicemail systems set up("Press one for Food Not Bombs, Press two for Freaks With Guns, etc....") I knew a few people but most of the places I was calling I didn't know anyone. Even though our cities are very close to one another, there isn't an awful lot of networking going between the two and most of my connections were within the punk community. I did a lot of button pushing and talking to machines. Two: Although everyone was pretty friendly and helpful, all the squatters seemed wary of the idea that a whole bunch of people were going to show up in their town for a week and had invited people from all over the country to join them. It seemed there was a lot of tension with the neighbors because they were having the same kind of gentrifuckation problems we were and I kept hearing this story over and over again about some group called Everybody's Kitchen who had set up a camp next to the Ⓐ Space to serve food and hang out and somehow managed to piss a lot of people off and outstay their welcome. I had to do a lot of convincing that we weren't a bunch of mooching hippies and that we were going to try our hardest not to piss off the neighbors.

I figured out about a week beforehand that the woman who Arrow had put as the contact for Philadelphia A) didn't live at the number she gave him; B)didn't really know anything about the festival; and C) was planning to leave town before we even showed up. This did not seem to fare well for our supposed branching out communication network. I heard there were some people from the squatter community who wanted to talk to a "representative" of the Nomadic Festival.

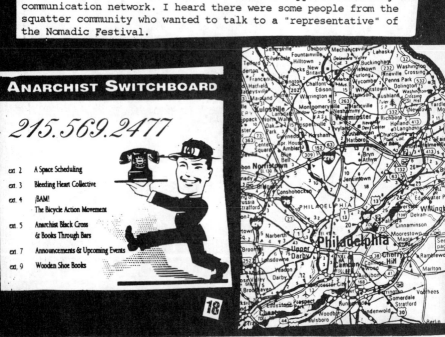

ANARCHIST SWITCHBOARD

215.569.2477

ext. 2	A Space Scheduling
ext. 3	Bleeding Heart Collective
ext. 4	¡BAM! The Bicycle Action Movement
ext. 5	Anarchist Black Cross & Books Through Bars
ext. 7	Announcements & Upcoming Events
ext. 9	Wooden Shoe Books

18

Alright. So I'm sitting shotgun in Blackbox with Pete, it's the day after the 13th Street evictions and there's a big picture of Cheese on the front page of the New York Times, we're lost in New Jersey, and I'm thinking about what I'm possibly going to say to these people I don't even know about who "we" are and what we "do." It was tricky and pretty funny at the same time.

I think it was the first time I felt this feeling that I got pretty used to over the course of the summer and finally learned to ignore. It was this feeling that we were teetering on the edge of a cliff, a whole bunch of people about to travel around together, not really knowing what our goal was except that we were going to make it around the country. We had all these supplies & a whole lot of collective talent, but we didn't have anything that we actually did as a group. Usually when people travel around as a group with dates set up and a bunch of stuff it's because they play in a band or they have a dance troupe or something. For all the time we spent setting up a schedule and travel route - the whole thing was still pretty amorphous and mysterious, especially to us. We were trying to break new ground - inspire people to hit the road and travelers to organize and build autonomous communities - see if we could do it ourselves building on the framework of anarchist groups and pockets of resistance we knew scattered throughout the country. We sent all these zines out to people all over the country telling them we were showing up in their town and to be prepared - but what were we going to do? The fact was until we all showed up in Philly we had never even all hung out as a group - much less worked together on a project. Me and Arrow talked pretty loud about how we were going to have parades in every town and blow up police

SWIMMING IN THE LOGAN SQUARE FOUNTAIN

stations and shit. But we didn't have any money and we had a whole lot of people expecting us to show up and entertain them or at least a whole lot of people wondering what the fuck we were all about. A recipe for disaster? Maybe.

Philadelphia was the first stop on our list and nothing was
organized except that Moth and Judith were going to hook us up
with some organic vegetables and we could have a party at the
KillTime warehouse. It was a funny week. We pulled it off pretty
well with the help of some of the West Philly Anarchists. The
first night we showed up at the Ⓐ Space, Josie let us all stay at
the Ben Fletcher Community Center, an old shoe warehouse that had
been abandoned since the early 70's and had just been reopened by
a group of Wobblies. It was this pretty dilapidated building with
boxes and boxes of shoes lining the walls and an old style
printing press. We all slept on the roof.

The next day we got a bunch of food and all cooked together.
There was this car that showed up to travel with us: this old
hippie guy Dennis, this girl Dizzy and her dog Trouble, and these
two horrible deadheads who were disappointed to find out that
Arrow was not their old rainbow brother Shooting Arrow or
something really lame like that. They left pretty quickly, Dennis
caravaned with us till Newport, Kentucky, but got fed up with us
(he was totally crazy though, the voices in his head told him to
come with us..), and Dizzy and Trouble traveled with us till
Austin. Not the throngs of people we expected to show up, but it
was a start.

Diana and Stacey got the city of Philadelphia to give them a
bunch of paint (it was some anti-graffiti pawn group I think) and
we painted a mural around the corner from the Ⓐ Space. Me and
Pete and a couple people reworked this malt liquor billboard
right above the mural one night so that it was an ad warning of
the dangers of drugs (at the last minute we realized we had no
wheatpaste but we got the key to the food co-op and made paste
out of organic buckwheat flour which didn't hold so great.) We
cooked a lot of food where ever we could and ate big meals
together. We all hung out in Rittenhouse square and caused a
ruckus. A bunch of us swam in this huge fountain one day. We
hooked up the CB's in Black Box and Red Thunder. We camped in
Fairmount park one night with the 5005 squat crew.

The main strip of squats in West Philadelphia is on Baltimore
Avenue and that's where we spent most of our time, hanging out at
the Ⓐ Space, talking about our plans for the summer. We all split
up to sleep - some folks stayed at the Ben Fletcher warehouse,
some people stayed at Butthook Manor, some people stayed in the
lot next to Ⓐ Space, some people stayed at Notsquat, and some of
us stayed at the no longer existant Stayfree Squat. Even though
we didn't have a whole lot of things organized, the local Philly
people were curious and helpful and it was obvious we weren't out
to ruin anyone's life and after a few days we had made a bunch of
new friends.

HELLOW --- WELCOLM TO THE

NOMADIC FESTIVAL

PHILADELPHIA WEEKEND

OPEN YOUR SENSES WIDE, AND BRING YOUR CREATIVITY TO

○ KiLL-TiME ○
WAREHOUSE
(ON LANGCASTER BETWEEN 31st · 38th)
FRIDAY, JUNE 9th
FOR A COSTUMED CHAOS
PARTY

ORIGINAL SILKSCREEN DESIGNS

A NIGHT OF LIVE MUSIC, PER-
FORMANCE ART, VIDIOS, FOOD
AND SENSUALITY. PLEASE
BRING MASKS, COSTUMES, AND
PSYCHOACTIVE MINDS !!!

CLARK PARK
ON BALTIMORE AND 44th ST
SATURDAY, JUNE 10th
FOR AN OPEN-MIC STYLE
OUTDOOR FESTIVAL!

ANARCHIST LITERATURE AND FANZINES

LOCAL ARTISTS, POETS, MUSICIANS
PERFORMERS INVITED TO SHOW
OFF. SHOW STARTS AT 3.00 PM
BOTH EVENTS ARE FREE BUT
DONATIONS WILL BE ASKED FOR

That Friday night, Eric hosted a party for us at KillTime and a lot
people showed up. Stacey was painting faces and we broke out the
costume trunk which had been collecting dust all week in the back o
Red Thunder. Eric's band Downboy played with a bunch of other bands
all these people were dancing. There's something really intense and
powerful in the air when a whole room full of people are dancing
together. Everyone dances differently, some more reserved and
restrained, some more wild and chaotic. But I always notice that
there's this tendency to dance like the people immediately surround
you and after a while of sweating and getting down, everyone's styl
start to blend into each other and it's just one collective mass of
energy moving in unison. Dancing's really important to anything, I
think anyway.

There were a couple people who got up on the open mic and ranted for
while once the alcohol started to kick in on the crowd. There was th
guy who we had invited down from Circus Apocalypse in Pittsburgh -
Andrew the Impaled - who blew everyone's mind. He got up and ranted
a bit and then he breathed some fire. But then he did this crazy thin
where he shoved a screwdriver straight through his nose and people we
bugging out. Circus freaks are a breed unto themselves and I don't
always understand what drives them to do the stuff they do, but I do
have to say they have this great way of messing with people's heads.

It went on for hours. I have this foggy early morning drunken memory of all these people hanging out in the living room, having this wild jam with empty beer bottles and spoons. It was a good party.

On Saturday, a bunch of folks showed up from New York and we all hung out in Clark Park and had a big silkscreening get together but it was pretty low key cause most of us were still wiped out from the night before. Everyone just kind of hung out on the grass, waiting for something to happen that never materialized.

MAXIMIZE POTENTIAL FOR EMERGENCE

It was the end of a pretty slow week. We were just getting to know each other and we were all realizing that finding food and shelter can take up a lot of time and energy if you're with a bunch of people. We had all traveled before, but never with a whole posse and there wasn't too much focus to anything we were doing. The Philadelphia folks had been pretty welcoming to us, all things considered, but I couldn't help feeling frustrated at our lack of independence and reliance on our hosts. There were already a lot of questions brewing in my mind about what kind of concrete things we were going to put back into all these communities we planned on visiting over the course of the summer. I really wanted to see a lot more emphasis given to building stuff and making crafts, people bartering and teaching each other skills. I wanted us to help foster some kind of stable symbiotic relationship between radical travelers and radical communities, create bonds that would eventually bring us all more autonomy and freedom. The potential was there, but we seemed to keep getting caught up in a mix of basic survival mode and chaos party mode. It was the beginning of the Summer.

When we left the next Monday for Pittsburgh, we said our goodbyes, Stephanie went back to New York and we brought Andrew the Impaled, this guy Alexis, Dennis, Dizzy, and Trouble the dog along for the ride.

THE SHOW

This is what happened: losing each other on the highway in the first ten minutes after we left Philadelphia, we met up at the Circus Apocalypse house of Sin in Pittsburgh, where we camped out for a day and a half. Arrow called his friend Jill in Newport, Kentucky and she told him we could all sleep in her backyard and then she told him she had set up a "show" for us in downtown Cincinnati that Friday night at a pizza parlor. This, of course, was very funny because we didn't have a "show" and furthermore (as we found out), she had put really nice flyers all over town advertising "The Dropout Circus - A Carnival of Chaos!" and told all her friends how great we were.

So I guess it was Monday afternoon and we were all sitting in this coffee shop in South Pittsburgh trying to brainstorm something. We came up with a couple little skits and different ideas to freak out and entertain and educate the audience and we decided to leave the next morning and drive to Yellow Springs, home of Antioch College and supposedly a big field where we could all camp out to work on our "show" in the peace and tranquillity of rural Ohio.

We all split up to gather supplies and food and meet back at the house. Meanwhile, our host David Apocalypse taught Arrow and Stacey the basics of breathing fire and Ryan and Pete sewed together some juggling balls out of canvas and lentils. We dumpstered some big tin drums and a lot of vegetables. The Pittsburgh Food Not Bombs house kicked us down a bunch of bagels. I shuffled around a lot of papers and sent out the last of the zines before we took off.

YELLOW SPRINGS

After a night of meeting up with Scotty and a bunch of the Dayton clan, drinking a lot of beer, and constantly getting kicked out of spots we tried to camp, we all woke up in that mythical big field on the Antioch campus - groggy and sleep deprived in the early afternoon sun. It was Wednesday and we had our big show looming over our heads. Stacey painted this big Carnival of Chaos banner. Martine wrote a makeshift play about the eviction of the squats in New York and disco dancing squatters called Liberty Street. Pete and Ryan practiced their stickfighting. Arrow wrote a poem. Dizzy and Diana, inspired by a video Andrew the Impaled showed them, decided to dress up really fancy and eat worms (they went digging in the field for their prey.) Stacey and Arrow built fire sticks and practiced their fire breathing. I went off under a tree and wrote a rant I'd read for the introduction.

As the sun was going down we split up into cops and squatters
and did a run through of Martine's play and as much of the rest
of the show we could practice. We found this amphitheater on
the campus and did it all there, taking turns watching each
other and performing - drumming our oil cans on the sidelines
and cheering for each other. This was Do It Yourself theater if
any of us had ever seen it. Our show was in two days and we
hoped no one would notice that we didn't know what the fuck we
were doing.

NEWPORT

        Newport, Kentucky is right over the bridge from
Cincinnati and is a lovely town of Smut and Whisky. There are
all these laws regulating alcohol and nudity in Ohio, so
everyone goes over to the strip clubs and liquor stores across
the water. We all showed up on Thursday (I had to hitchhike cause I
went off to find a friend of mine in Yellow Springs and got left behind when
everyone got kicked out of the field and went to Dayton. I got a ride with these
hippies and then this Jesus freak who talked my ears off and it was ugly but
that's a whole other tale in itself.) with two other cars full of Dayton
and New York folks and hung out in Jill and Cecelie's backyard
drinking and causing a ruckus. Somehow Ryan got arrested (when I
asked Scotty what Ryan got arrested for he slurred: "drunken
intoxication") and the poor guy spent three days in the tank
while we all worked on the show. The cop's showed up at Jill and
Cecelie's house early in the morning to find fifteen passed out
dirty kids in the backyard. Cecelie managed to scare them off
because she is totally badass and we woke up and made pancakes.
We spent Friday riding around and dumpstering a lot of junk and
building stuff in the yard. We had this plan that we were going
to start the show by creating a sculpture out of dead TV's,
VCR's, pink flamingos - whatever we could find in the trash -
and then smash it all to pieces - recreating it all into
something else during the course of the show. It was our theme
of destruction and creation. Everyone made props - pig noses to
differentiate the cops from the squatters, masks. I stole a huge
Jolly Roger pirate flag from a big costume shop in Cincinnati,
we practiced Martine's play again. Ate a big dinner out of
Jill's garden and waited for nighttime.

SHITLOADS OF SOUL BUT NO TIME TO MEMORISE OUR LINES

        This was the thing: one of the reasons I was so hyped on
the idea of the Nomadic Festival to begin with was that I had
seen a million punk shows and touring bands and I was really
interested in doing something different with all the energy put
into traveling around and making a scene. Stages are a really
powerful thing and I've always liked the idea of being able to
break down the barriers between the performers and the audience
cause it's really hard not to somehow feel alienated watching a
spectacle that you're not a part of - have no role in creating.

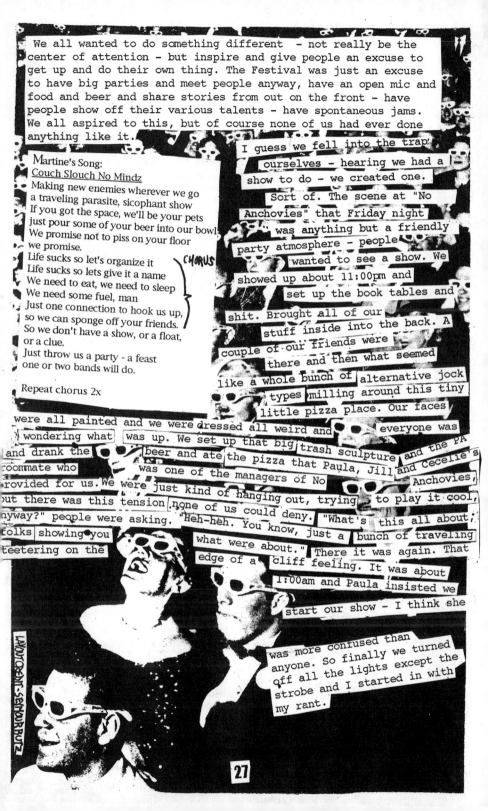

We all wanted to do something different - not really be the center of attention - but inspire and give people an excuse to get up and do their own thing. The Festival was just an excuse to have big parties and meet people anyway, have an open mic and food and beer and share stories from out on the front - have people show off their various talents - have spontaneous jams. We all aspired to this, but of course none of us had ever done anything like it.

Martine's Song:
Couch Slouch No Mindz

Making new enemies wherever we go
a traveling parasite, sicophant show
If you got the space, we'll be your pets
just pour some of your beer into our bowl
We promise not to piss on your floor
we promise.
Life sucks so let's organize it
Life sucks so lets give it a name   CHORUS
We need to eat, we need to sleep
We need some fuel, man
Just one connection to hook us up,
so we can sponge off your friends.
So we don't have a show, or a float,
or a clue.
Just throw us a party - a feast
one or two bands will do.

Repeat chorus 2x

I guess we fell into the trap ourselves - hearing we had a show to do - we created one. Sort of. The scene at "No Anchovies" that Friday night was anything but a friendly party atmosphere - people wanted to see a show. We showed up about 11:00pm and set up the book tables and shit. Brought all of our stuff inside into the back. A couple of our friends were there and then what seemed like a whole bunch of alternative jock types milling around this tiny little pizza place. Our faces were all painted and we were dressed all weird and everyone was wondering what was up. We set up that big trash sculpture and the PA and drank the beer and ate the pizza that Paula, Jill and Cecelie's roommate who was one of the managers of No Anchovies provided for us. We were just kind of hanging out, trying to play it cool, but there was this tension none of us could deny. "What's this all about, anyway?" people were asking. "Heh-heh. You know, just a bunch of traveling folks showing you what were about." There it was again. That teetering on the edge of a cliff feeling. It was about 1:00am and Paula insisted we start our show - I think she was more confused than anyone. So finally we turned off all the lights except the strobe and I started in with my rant.

27

Hell-o - welcome to our party. Some of you know us
some of you don't/some of you know some of us/some of us know some
of you/some of us don't even know ourselves let alone you or we or they
or us or them or it or anything - shit: We don't even really exist. We're
performing for you but you don't exist either - so we can't fuck up. It's
just us.

We all grew us in this twisted nightmare of a million spectacles and had
our roles planned out for us. We all watched way to much television. All
did our time in school - staring one way at a black bored and a droning
face. All had our share of stupid jobs - waking up to the same gray reality
every day. It's all in you. It's all in me. It doesn't go away. All that shit. All
that force fed information. All those decade old obscure Saturday
morning cereal commercial jingles. All those glossy billboards on the
highway. It's all festering in your head somewhere. It's our culture. It's
our Coca-cola McDonalds burger and fries fast food culture. It's our
nutrasweetbileball light FM ten day crash tabloid puke diet culture. It's
our reach out and touch someone with fiber optic cables and strangle
them to death Hallmark holiday culture. It's our Superman,
Supermarket, Superbowl, Super Stop and Shop freshandcleanandbright
and White Culture. It's our TV fucklore glossy eyesore sex and death
headlines at the check out counter consuming your face culture.It's our
Nintendo war - let's sweep the dirt under our new sofa honey and let it
rot and overflow until it eats our dog culture.It's our wage slave/time
clock Winston weekends get drunk with your buddies to forget you
have to go back to work on Monday lazychair Budweiser culture. It's our
cheap holiday in other people's misery get away vacation travel package
get me the fuck out of this horrible empty life culture. It's our stick your
fucked up kids in our mental hospitals and we'll force feed them prozac
and xanax and ritalin and thorazine and haldol and some shit you never
even heard of and we'll make them productive members of society
nightmare medication culture.It's our sit back, relax, and enjoy the show
- Sesame Street to MTV I have the attention span of a flee sound byte
flicker hollywood Imagine Nation I'm so fucking bored mall-rat shit
culture. It's our let's sell you a bunch of soul less plastic trash and sell it
back to you ten years later as nostalgia lost and tired culture. It's our
horrible golden arches cop show game show entertainment culture -
spreading like some mutant disease around the entire world with a few
greedy fuckers behind the stage raking in the cash and taking us all
down with them. Fuck all that.

Have you ever noticed how our American culture has this way of sucking
the soul out of every good, original idea, every beautiful work of art it
can get its grubby hands on, every person with something to say -
somehow coopting and selling and rehashing them all until what was
once full of life becomes an empty shell, a musak reenactment, a
corporate theme song, a symbol of death? Have you ever noticed how
our American culture somehow manages to channel any desire for
rebellion or change into a desire for somepiece of consumer trash?
Tonight we're going to do things a little differently. Forget everything
you ever learned about being entertained. Tonight, with our total
unprofessionalness and clumsiness, lack of tack or talent, shitloads of
soul but no time to memorize our lines - right here in this very room
we're going to destroy the barriers between us and you and create
something beautiful in its place. This is our traveling outlaw party - our
feedback circus - live here tonight then disappearing onto the highway
for destinations unknown.

This is our party. This is your party. Now we're gonna burn it down....

28

CULT OF DOMESTICITY BY DENNIS

I felt like Malcolm Maclaren must have felt at one of those
first Sex Pistols shows - all these people show up and it's just
a bunch of guys on stage who can't play their instruments making
a lot of noise. I finished my rant urging the crowd to get up
and destroy shit (someone told me later this guy tried to smash
the strobe light and Dizzy kicked him away) and Pete came out
dressed as a cop with a black mask on yelling at everyone to
stay back. Ryan was in jail, so Danny (his understudy) came out
with a stick and they fought - Pete defending the trash monolith
we had created. Danny knocked him down and we all came out from
the back howling and screaming and totally smashed the sculpture
to bits. Then Arrow read his "Endarchy" poem and we all
scattered into the bewildered crowd chanting in unison "We each
have a stone." Then Danny and Diana played this guitar/flute
medley that was pretty and Martine tied up a naked Pete and
poured hot wax all over his body. We all played drums as Stacey
and Arrow danced around and breathed fire. The crowd didn't
really seem phased: when all else fails - try shock value. Dizzy
chickened out so Diana and this girl from Dayton ate worms.
Danny took a hammer and hammered a nail into the head of his
dick. "Who wants to see me hammer this fucking nail into my
fucking dick?!" I recall him saying. Spectacle extrodinare. By
the end the whole thing was totally ridiculous - smashed up
appliances everywhere, a lot of confused people, Danny trying to
look like he wasn't in a lot of pain, poor Paula freaking out
cause we had scratched up the floor and made a royal mess -
apparently for no reason at all except that we were obviously
crazed and needed gas money. The energy pretty much died and we
decided not to even do Martine's play. After everyone left we
were still inside cleaning up everything we had messed up. At
the time it felt like we had fallen off that cliff. But again,
it was a start.

NASHVILLE - CONCLUSION TO THIS STRANGE TA

We kept going. Hung out in Newport for another day and
said our goodbyes. Got Ryan out of jail. We started driving at
about noon and by the time we hit Nashville we realized we were
almost totally broke. It was Sunday evening, June 18th. Being
the historian and all I can safely say that it was a turning
point for the whole Nomadic Festival because it was that night
we discovered we could use the talents we had been practicing
all week together for a less noble purpose: to hustle. We found
the main strip - packed full of drunk tourists and frat boys and
we broke it all out. Fire, juggling, dancing, playing drums,
Danny did a few piercings- everything we had been practicing for
our show was a great way to make money on the street. I went
around and scammed pizza and chinese food from the closing shops
and scouted for The Man while people went around with the bucket
and collected gas funds. After a couple hours of standing
outside "Hooters" we had more than enough money to get to
Atlanta. Morale was high and we all slept at a friend of Diana's
house to rest up. It was the first time everything had really
clicked when we all worked together and it wasn't any
coincidence that the necessity of getting the hell out of
Nashville drove us to do it.

Wash Entrance

There's this power you have when you travel around with a big group of people. For all the shit you have to go through - finding places to stay, gathering food, getting everyone in the vans at the same time, trying not to get in too much trouble - there are those days when it's totally worth it. The best times we had that first month weren't when we showed up for a scheduled stop. It was when we'd pull into some gas station somewhere and all pile out like it was that

DIZZY + MARTINE TAKE A MAKESHIFT SHOWER

act in the circus when all the clowns keep getting out of the car, Blue Dog and Trouble leading the way.. We'd roam the isle's of the convience stores, freaking out anyone in the general vicinity, Dizzy stealing cigarettes for everyone, Ryan checking the dumpsters, us all looking like we were going to set up camp in the parking lot, and then leaving very quickly.

THE NOMADIC SODA BANDITS CAPER

The day after we left Nashville, we woke up about 60 miles North of Atlanta on some back road in Georgia. We'd had a shitty time trying to find a camping ground and after hours of driving in the dark, finally found a bunch of trees that didn't look like they were on private property, so we pulled off. Our plan for the day was to find a camping spot next to a lake and swim and cook food and work on our performance. Stopped at the Wal-Mart in town (or in the strip-mall, I don't think there was a town) to get some supplies and everytime one of us would venture into a new section there would be this voice over the loud speaker "Security Check in Section 16 - All Cameras Scan and Record." It was so funny.

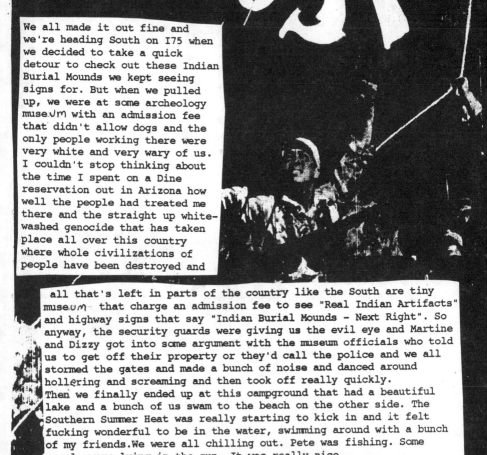

We all made it out fine and we're heading South on I75 when we decided to take a quick detour to check out these Indian Burial Mounds we kept seeing signs for. But when we pulled up, we were at some archeology museum with an admission fee that didn't allow dogs and the only people working there were very white and very wary of us. I couldn't stop thinking about the time I spent on a Dine reservation out in Arizona how well the people had treated me there and the straight up white-washed genocide that has taken place all over this country where whole civilizations of people have been destroyed and

all that's left in parts of the country like the South are tiny museum that charge an admission fee to see "Real Indian Artifacts" and highway signs that say "Indian Burial Mounds - Next Right". So anyway, the security guards were giving us the evil eye and Martine and Dizzy got into some argument with the museum officials who told us to get off their property or they'd call the police and we all stormed the gates and made a bunch of noise and danced around hollering and screaming and then took off really quickly.
Then we finally ended up at this campground that had a beautiful lake and a bunch of us swam to the beach on the other side. The Southern Summer Heat was really starting to kick in and it felt fucking wonderful to be in the water, swimming around with a bunch of my friends. We were all chilling out. Pete was fishing. Some people were lying in the sun. It was really nice.
Here's where the story gets crazy: Me and Stacey decide to go up to the soda machines on the hill and try the warm salt water trick. For those of you who don't know, the warm salt water trick is a simple way to get a bit of extra pocket change and a bunch of soda by short-circuiting the soda machine mechanism through it's dollar slot with a squirt bottle full of liquid. I guess the water acts as an electricial conductor which fucks up the system. A lot of companies are pretty hip to this by now and have found ways to secure their machines. We tried this at various rest stops along the ways and had minimal success: a couple cans here and there, a few quarters. But mostly that was because there were other people around and we didn't really have the chance to milk them for all they were worth.
But me and Stacey were alone on top of this hill. Just us, the machines, and Ryan's bike bottle. We tried the first one and it just shut off. Then we tried the brand new, sparkling, Fruitopia machine.

I hate Fruitopia. First of all, they're owned by the evil Coca-Cola
monolithic world rapists. Second of all, their loud
pseudopsychedelic soundbyte marketing campaign directed at hip 90's
youth made me want to puke everytime I saw one of those ads last
summer. Third, the stuff tastes like shit. Anyway, we squirted a
bunch of water in and the thing just made this weird noise and then
it started to shake and spit up a couple quarters. Then we started
hitting the buttons and all this Fruitopia started coming out - can
after can. Stacey ran down the hill and told everyone. It was a
fantasy come true. Within a couple minutes we had a line of people
moving up and down the hill with boxes full of cans that said things
like: "Strawberry Passion Awarness" and "Tangerine Aura Whatever the
Fuck." We must have had more than a hundered cans and we figured we
could sell them at the beach or something. Everyone was scrambling
to get packed up so we could leave the scene of the crime. Someone
must have ratted on us though. Just as we were about to drive off,
two cop cars showed up and blocked our path. We were freaking out
bad. But Arrow played it really cool. He put on this syrupy southern
drawl and said right to the cops face: "I don't know what happened
officer. Me and my buddy went up to get a Coke and next thing we
knew the machine was spittin' out cans like it was Vegas..." He gave
the cop a couple cans and a big apologetic smile, which seemed to
satisfy the guy, and then we drove off, slowly at first, and then
really fast. The fucking Nomadic Soda Bandits.
So as soon as we got out of the county, we pulled off the highway
to a strip mall. We were all starving. None of us had eaten all day
and the Fruitopia and just the whole state of affairs was making us
all giddy. But we were still broke. It just so happened that there
was a Taco Bell, a Pizza Hut, a Kentucky Fried Chicken, and a
Burger King all right next to each other (fancy that.) Just like we
had been doing it for years, we all split up and each of us either
went to a dumpster or went inside Fast Food Hell and tried the
wrong order scam ("When I ordered my pizza yesterday I didn't order

any mushrooms and I *hate* mushrooms! That's right. Yesterday. About
2:00pm. No problem. Large with extra cheese - thank you. - I'll be
outside digging through your old breadsticks with my scummy
friends.") Everone else gathered burritos and chicken and biscuits
and cornbread and burgers and a couple minutes later we regrouped
in the parking lot and had a feast off the wastes of modern
capitalist society and washed it all down with our bevrage pillage
of the day. There was this feeling in the air that we could get
away with anything. When you're hungry and delerious, fast food
trash tastes like the best stuff you've ever eaten. I did something
I never though I'd ever do in a million years - I ate a bunch of
KFC chicken nuggets out of the dumpster - and liked it. It started
raining and we took it as a sign to leave, so we made the journey
into Atlanta and pulled in at about dusk.

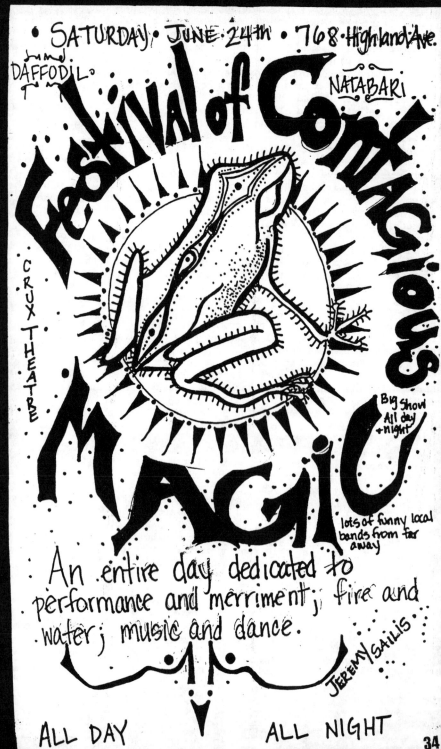

· SATURDAY · JUNE 24th · 768 · Highland Ave.

DAFFODIL

Festival of Contagious MAGIC

NATABARI

CRUX THEATRE

Big Show
All day
+ night

lots of funny local
bands from far
away

An entire day dedicated to performance and merriment; fire and water; music and dance.

JEREMY SAILIS

ALL DAY   ALL NIGHT

34

festiVAl of
SAturday June 24 1995

768 Highland

DAFFODIL
NATABARI
CRUX THEATRE
Jeremy
Sailis
much
more.

fire
stilts
puppets
noise
food
chaos

Contagious Magic

We stumbled right into the middle of a really strange scene that week in Atlanta that left my head spinning by the time we left. I spent a lot of time that week thinking about potential. I was carrying around firecrackers in my pocket all the time and there was always all this bread lying around that never got eaten.

It really all started last Winter in New Orleans when I met these women from this dance troupe Natabari on the street and gave them a Nomad Fest flyer and then Tonya, part of the Natabari clan, wrote a letter to Arrow inviting us out to Georgia to check out what they had going on and come work together.

We were all pretty excited cause it was the first place we were heading where there was land for us to stay and stuff set up and none of us had ever been there before. Tonya and a bunch of people had worked hard and had set up a four day festival coinciding with our arrival that had workshops and parties and food and parades and all this really great shit.

We were staying in North-East Atlanta; what looked like an old commercial district - a lot of abandoned warehouses - artist groups popping up everywhere. It was really close to the main drag, hangout spot - Little Five Points, which seemed to be part of the rainbow circuit - lots of people passing through.

Where we were actually staying was a place called The Compound - a fenced off piece of land with surveillance cameras at the gate, a group of people who had the appearance of being hippies but were actually part of the Millitia movement and had these survivalist, kind of "new patriot" politics where they didn't want government intervention in anything they did and were really concerned with their rights as "American Citizens." Not anarchists by any means, we had some common ground and they treated us really well, though they were always talking about these crazy New World Order conspiracies and had combat training in the back yard.

35

ZIMO + THE WATERMELON

Arrow, Your Nom. Fest. flyer was passed on to me by a traveling friend in New Orleans and I am interested.

I have been living in Atlanta for about two years working with the dance group Natabari and on occasion working with the dance group Daffodil. This is- we are- an eclectic group of thinkers and performers. We like action.

Since I was a kid, I've been enthralled by the gypsy lifestyle and within this last year I have been learning how to make this dream happen. The main ingredient to any thickening plot is ...ACTION.

We are a network of ACT-ers With as many agendas as there are personalities. There are approximately 30 kids in varying states of vagabonding fluxuation who claim affiliation with either Daffodil or Natabari.

I am a chameleon. I like bikes and other forms of "live" transportation. I'm down with the revolution just so long as I can dance. One major dream I have is to go to NYC. As in be INVOLVED.

I mainly dance with the group, but any street performing is fun especially when there are hand drums.

THIS LETTER'S MAIN OBJECTIVE IS TO ENCOURAGE YOU! to go, man, go with the flow of the traveling vibe, bring it to Atlanta and we can get live. We have much to learn, much to do, Tanya, Atlanta, GA

The Natabari house was a few blocks away and was a totally different scene. It was a couple dozen folks, really tight knit clan of artists - painters, sculptors, dancers, musicians, writers, all very serious about their work. Their performances were extremely well crafted and painstakingly choreographed, rehearsed for hours with the goal of perfection. Very spiritual in nature, their clan held rituals honoring various goddesses and gods and they studied and incorporated dance and music from all over the world.

The Nom Fest and the Natabari clan were two very different groups of people from very different backrounds with what seemed like different ends in mind. We were mostly harsh city folk, profane and angry, drank a lot of beer and wanted to fuck shit up. They were much more laid back, woke up every morning and practiced Yoga together, smoked a lot of pot, worked on their art. We came from the squats and the anarchist travelers circuit, we knew about fighting off police and surving from the trash. They came from a more stable place without the same kind of confrontation and obviously had more connections to the

NOMADIC FESTIVAL
JUNE 21 - 24

WED 21. WORKSHOPS
3:30 - LOU ANNE - HERBOLOGY
4PM - PAUL - RUNES
4:30 - 6:30 ALANA - FACIALS, MASSAGES, & TAROT
8PM - SOLSTICE DRUM CIRCLE

THURS 22.
11 PM - MUD BATH
4 PM - MUD PEOPLE PARADE DOWNTOWN ATLANTA
8 PM - RAINBOW SWEAT LODGE

FRI 23.
5 PM - DECORATION PARTY
7 PM - L5P PARADE WALK 'N BIKE
8 PM - FREE FOOD IN L5P SQUARE
COMPOUND PARTY - BANDS AND DJ'S 10 PM

SAT 24.
12 NOON - BIZARRE BAZAAR CARNIVAL FEATURING:
NATABARI DANCERS, CRUX THEATRE, VARIOUS SIDE
SHOWS, FIRE BREATHERS, FLEA MARKET, HAIR WRAPS

FROM I-20, TAKE MORELAND AVE. NORTH
LEFT ON EUCLID, RIGHT ON WASHITA, LEFT ON
NORTH HIGHLAND, 1/3 MILE ON THE RIGHT.

FROM I-75/85, EXIT 96, TURN LEFT ON BOULE-
VARD, TAKE FIRST RIGHT ON HIGHLAND, 1/2 MILE
ON LEFT.

768 HIGHLAND AVE.
THE COMPOUND

ATLANTA
LITTLE FIVE POINTS

rainbow travelers circuit and the deadhead scene. To us, performance was something new we were learning about along the way and it always seemed to come out abrasive and crude, a reflection of the hateful world we were coming from and maybe an attempt to shake people out of the fantasy that everything was alright. To them, performance was everything and they strived for beauty and trancendence over anything else. I think we had a lot to learn from each other.

Despite all the differences, there was intermingling between the tribes and we pretty much spent the week back and forth between the two houses and Little Five Points, setting up the show and hanging out. In the morning some of us would wake up and practice yoga over at the Natabari pad. There were some good workshops the first day. We got a lot of food kickdowns and we'd all cook and eat together. People painted and built things together, took acid and baked bread, silkscreened and made masks. Me and Supa and Ignatz, masters of propaganda, went off to co-conspire on various world takeover plots. The festivities were nightly at The Compound and there were always lot of people around building fires, dancing and playing drums.

THE PARADE IN LITTLE 5 POINTS

But we really were coming at things fro different perspectiv and when it came dow it I think a lot of people didn't know w to make of each othe. We had this parade through the streets Atlanta and Tonya dr up this beautiful but kind of confusing fl: telling people we we:

having a feast at the end of the parade but it never really materialized. In fact, it seemed like a lot of the things we tried to do fell through one way or another. The mud bath fell through due to lack of mud, the sweat lodge fell through due to lack of sweat put in to setting it up, and the show that Saturday night could only be called a chaotic disaster. I guess we just didn't mix right with the Daffodil clan. Most of those guys stayed far away from the festival while it was going on all week, only showing up to perform their fire and water dance at the Saturday gathering. There were a lot of people around The Compound that night and all day there had been various performances and side shows taking place. We obviously didn't have the most well rehearsed, beautiful show, but it was ours and we had worked hard all week putting it together. We did Martine's squatter play and Arrow spoke passionately afterwards about our community back East and the threat of eviction all the

buildings face. I did my culture rant thing and we smashed a whole bunch of TV's and set off fireworks. It was going well and we had good energy but all of a sudden I look down by the other side of The Compound and the Daffodil clan are lighting their torches and beating drums. Whatever good connections we had made with the Natabari folks all week seemed to go up in smoke in a matter of minutes. Everyone who was watching our show walked over to check out the fire dance and we were left feeling really stupid, cut off half way through our act. It wasn't really that our show was so important, it wasn't - it was the fact that all week we had been learning from these people, checking out their scene and what they all did, and when it came time for us to show them what we were about, it didn't seem like it really mattered to them at all.

Let's Eat

NOW
GO!

Springvale Lakeside Park

Springvale Park Sunfest

8PM

38

A Nomadically Supported, Natabari encouraged, Starving Artist Hosted, Foot & foo est Bread thanks: Highland Bagel in Caribu Coff w/Highland & Savananda Bakery.

NATABARI

I went over and checked out what Daffodil were doing and it was this beautiful ritual - a fight between the gods of fire and water - intense and powerful - spitting flames and extinguishing them with spraying water. They obviously were very good at what they did and knew it. In the background I could hear Dizzy yelling all drunk over the microphone: "Come on - who wants to see me eat these worms? Come on - I'm really gonna do it." Just then I felt that smashing head first into the bottom of a cliff feeling again real bad. What the hell were we doing here? This was a bunch of performance artists who didn't care about anything else - why were we trying to play their game, anyway? I didn't know about this contagious magic shit. At the same time I felt totally alienated from our (drunk) (fucking stupid) crew and none of what we were doing really felt like it was getting anything accomplished and we were just kidding ourselves. What a mess.

The party pretty much dissolved and there was all this floating animosity and miscommunication all over the place so I just went on a long walk through the neighborhood by myself.

I finally came back to the set where we had performed and nobody was around. There were a bunch of punk kids I didn't know sitting behind the stage huffing all our gold spraypaint with glazed looks on their faces. One of them was trying to convince me that huffing paint actually activated psychic paths in the brain that didn't get used otherwise. Whatever, man. Beaten, I slunk off to my sleeping bag, figuring it would all be better in the morning.

CRUX THEATER

It poured the next day and we had a lot of stuff to clean up but people came by and helped. Over food and drink, things got patched up with the Natabari folks and we left with new friends, acknowledging the progress we had made together and talking about the future. It's pretty obvious now that we were all striving for the same goals in the end - freedom and community, the creation of beauty and autonomy from outside oppression. They really are their own separate subculture, have created a world for themselves outside the mainstream, carved a small pocket of rebellion for themselves in the middle of Georgia. It's a shame we didn't all explode, of each other like we should have but I for one learned a whole lot that week about trying to communicate and working together with different kinds of folks. Somehow in the misted of everything, we convinced a four person Atlanta crew (Tanya, Sean, Supa, and Kim) to hook up with us in New Mexico and travel around for a while. But damn, our gang left feeling slightly beaten, happy to be back on the road.

IGNATZ VS. THE TYPEWRITER

LYRICS BY dvtkiN @ badite.95

The children of this age have grown fat and placid. They can no longer appreciate the environment without color vision enhancement and diet cola pop refreshment. So many have lazily accepted the media reality. Shudder to think of returning to family values on the same agenda that is cutting artistic funding nation wide. So we have sought a sanctuary away from the society that values empty ideals at such a heavy price. When work supersedes artistic creation the soul withers. We need to create beauty for our selves!

Money is a representative of our distance from one another. It allows us to act as independent nations, rather that interdependent creatures of the biosphere. We speak in terms of organic truths: THE EARTH IS AS WE ARE : one organism. Like selfish children we rebel against our mother. For the gifts we have been graced with are requiring attention and respect.. as such we should treat each other.

Brothers and Sisters,

We as performers have chosen to free our minds from ignorant shackles and reach out to our immediate community in a theatrical sense. Yes! We perform to spread a live connection, sharing all that we have, and creating an atmosphere of paradise for you to enter as you will.

Nomadic Connection

Works by Lania Atanda

Illustrations by Sean Lee

① Born of inspiration, leaving ② Atlanta from Nomad Propaganda was a chore. The idea is reality. "Lets join them!" "Sure!" "Okay" "Cod..." "Lets go!"

our driver locked the keys in the car, ran out of gas, sucked her bikini

in the vacuum cleaner & dropped her conga on her foot. I'm surprised we made it outside the perimeter.

③ We stopped in New Orleans to Rustle up money by performing dance & drum. New orleans smells so bad in the summer, no body with much cash (or sense!) Vacations there. We made enough money for coffee & beniegs before we split.

Rolling onto the plains of Eastern New Mexico at 2am, the weather is perfect and the moon is full. Jason is awake... We do bong hits and drink tequila until the moon sinks, rippling in waves, into the horizon.

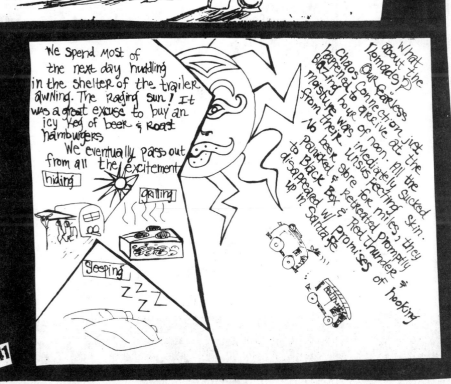

We spend most of the next day huddling in the shelter of the trailer awning. The Raging sun! It was a great excuse to buy an icy keg of beer & roast hamburgers

We eventually pass out from all the excitement.

hiding

grilling

sleeping

ZZZ

What about the Nomads? Our fearless Chaos Connection just happened to arrive at the boiling hour of noon. All the moisture was sucked immediately from their unsuspecting skin. Insulting, they retreated promptly to their store for miles. —No beer. Panicked & Red Thunder & Black Box & disappeared w/ promises of hooking up in Santa Fe.

Santa Fe Chvs

Santa fe was a misorganized party. An enshrouding band of 6 or more leather clad road warriors convinced the nomads to come to their show. Adam & fire session heated the towns summer night & lots o' kids raged

① We camped at Diablo Canyon that night. Some people stayed to drum while others looked for a party down the road. Kim passed out in a pile of ants ... ouch!

② The next day our vehicle: Sin Sek-1 split for Big Sur

③ Where we camped next to the ocean for 2 nights

The next stop is Eugene, OR.
Again, Food Not Bombs feeds & houses we insurgents. Primary agendas for Nomad Crue is finding Ickys Teahouse and preparing for Fridays show

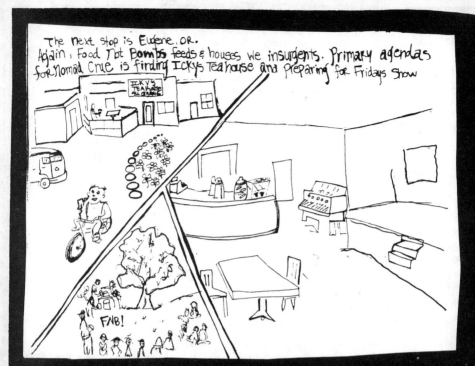

FNB!

The goony bird skit rocked!

Magically Inspired

PUPPETRY

AND FIRE!

the next day, FNB served outside the courthouse passing out literature about mumia while police filmed the activity

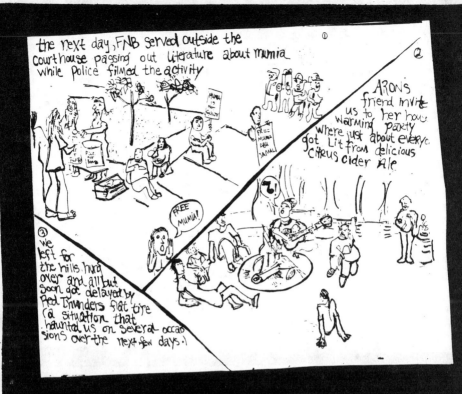

ARON's friend invite us to her house warming party where just about everyo. got Lit from delicious Citrus cider Ale

① ② ③

FREE MUMIA!

We left for the hills hund over and all but soon got delayed by Red Thunders flat tire (a situation that haunted us on several occasions over the next few days.)

The first night we camped at a mediocre hot springs illegally. We were awakened by a concerned hotspring cleaning volunteer, making us decide to find Cougar hotsprings soon. The Red Thunder flat tire syndrome strikes again, but after successfully pissing off the gas station attendant enough to threaten calling the cops on us, and robbing the supermarket of enough snacks for everyone (many thanks!), we head onward in working order. We were relaxing in the glorious Cougar Hotsprings in hours.

The next day we hit Portland in time to catch the last of the downtown hub bub. The "Powerhouse" gives an "okay" for 15 of us to stay at their home. Most of us are restless and go to the coffee shop section of town, but every place is closed. We make use of the empty streets to chalk drawings on the sidewalk.

And this is bringing us to an end to my part of the narration. Sim, Geck. One, better known as Kim & the Cohesives, leave Portland later that day but not before Food Not Bombs gathers us to the park. We exchange addresses and good byes ... we're off

Write to:
c/o SUPA
P.O. 5419
Atlanta, GA
30317

A Cheap Holiday in Eureka Springs

We left Atlanta almost as broke as when we showed up, determined to have a relaxing week in Arkansas before we hit Austin. By a very strange set of circumstances involving a crazy llama farmer lady friend of Arrow's and her racist joke telling boyfriend, we ended up without a place to stay, stuck in this tourist town - Eureka Springs. We hooked up with this guy Chuck who had a car with weird drawings and various Noam Chomsky quotes all over it. He also had a bullhorn which he'd use to broadcast to anyone in the general vicinity his thought's about the state of the world.

Luckily, we all found a really beautiful camping spot by this lake out of town and got to play in the woods and swim and relax for a couple days. But we didn't even have enough money to get to the border of Texas and had a lot of people expecting us to show up. Besides which, our camping spot was only going to last so long before the locals kicked us out and Eureka Springs was a nightmare.

It struck me like it must have been one of those 60's boomtowns - sleepy town in Northern Arkansas where a whole bunch of hippies moved to create their new world on the land but now it's just a bunch of old people who own boutiques and antique shops and fast food restaurants and just cater to a bunch of Fat American Tourists. So the entire economy is fueled by Summer Vacation and some myth of what a quaint American town should look like. Everyones' grandparents were there on holiday buying a bunch of little trash culture shit to put on their mantle pieces and windowsills and give to their relatives("Someone Went to Eureka Springs and All I Got Was This Stupid Fucking Shirt That's Going to Sit and Rot in the Back of My Closet Forever".)

It was horrible. We couldn't perform anywhere without getting hassled by the cops, everything was really expensive, and it was pretty clear we weren't wanted in the midst of this tourist bubble. It was a reality slap in the face that most Americans work 9 to 5 jobs they hate and then they take their two week "vacation" every year to get away from it all by buying meaningless stuff and doing what they're told is "relaxing".

The whole tourism industry is fucked, no two ways about it. The separation between work and leisure in this society creates this need for people to take a ritualized break in their routine and go somewhere else to do the same things they'd do at home. You'd think with all the amazing things to see and cultures to learn about in this world, people fortunate enough to travel would want to actually break out of their routines for a little while and experience different ways to live. But vacation for most is just a boring consumption fantasy, trying to forget the wage slave life they have to go back to and trying to block out the ticking clock in their head. But we're creatures of habit. That's why McDonalds makes so much money - because they're the same wherever you go and I reckon it's comforting when you see that sign on the highway and it makes you remember you can get a Big Mac and a Coke anywhere in the world and it will always taste the same.

Being unwillingly thrown into the middle of this horrendous carnival of Americana made me realize just how boring most people's lives really are. People in this country live out their adventure fantasies by watching bad Hollywood movies. People in this country drive for days with their families to get to the Grand Canyon and are secretly disappointed when they actually get there because it's just another picture snapped to show the neighbors back home. People in this country look at beautiful sunsets over the water and say they look just like postcards. What's happened to us?

Sitting in the main square in Eureka Springs trying to sell my patches, watching all the people walk by, the smell of funnel cakes and hamburgers in the air, I decided for probably the millionth time in my life that I hated America and everything it stood for. Looking at all the Fat American Tourists walking around with their cameras and blank stares threw me into a rage. It made me think about the sad state of this world threw with its legacy of imperialism and colonization where whole countries are forced into prostituting their culture and land to the same Fat American Tourists who come in droves every year to escape their lives in the "land of plenty." Sitting in the square, I suddenly recalled one of those old TV commercial jingles from when I was a kid that was hiding in the back of my brain somewhere:

"Come back to Jamaica - What's old is what's new. We want you to join us - We made it for you."

How could they have played that commercial so many times that I could still remember it years later and people didn't realize how fucked up it was? Did most people watching it really think that Jamaica was actually *made* for *them*, the privileged Americans? What are we doing here and where can we go to get away from all this?

Sitting with all my vagabond friends in the square, it seemed like a revolutionary act just to slip out of that work/leisure cycle and travel the way we were traveling - with no money, our travel as our work and all the leisure we could stomach. All these people wanted to do was get away from their lives, live out some fantasy of the American Dream for a little while. They traveled with expectations and goals, they knew what they wanted because they had seen it on television. We were explorers, checking out uncharted territory in the anarchist network, figuring things out for ourselves, learning every day, knee-deep in the American Reality.

The idea when you travel is to throw yourself into situations where you're forced to talk to people and figure out how to survive. See how people live in different places, try living that way yourself, blow your mind every chance you get, explore new places with an open mind and a true heart. It seemed we had explored Eureka Springs long enough and done enough soul searching to know we wanted to get the fuck out.

I guess it was bound to happen but we outstayed our welcome. Trying to make a couple extra dollars for gas, Pete ended getting thrown in jail for juggling outside some store and the cops were telling us his court date wasn't until the end of August and they might just deport his Canadian ass back up North anyway. It was all looking pretty grim until Martine got in touch with his mom and she wired us enough money to bail him out, buy him a beer, and make the drive to Austin as quickly as possible.

Usually when you fall under the custody of the state you've at least done someeething you knew could lead to trouble However there are instances such as being thrown in the drunk tank, or uhm .... well anyway in the drunk tank, you usually didn't see it coming, but it's only a night or so and then you're out hungry and hungover. Not a big deal. There're also the times when you expect to be detained as the result of a demo or blokade , again the outcome is fairly predictable. While you might be beaten you can expect to be out soon enough. It's the times when didn't see it coming and you don't know what to expect that really freak you out

Eureka spings is a small tourist town in the hills of the north west Arkansas not far from uncle Bills birthplace. Once a safe haven for hippies, freaks and alternative lifestylers it gave way to the capitalist 80's and degenerated into an idustryless town scrambling to survive. The streets , once a marketplace of local craftspeople and artists, are now lined with the scum of chinese mass produced trinkets and trash , rotting pogos and coors filled fat american fuck face Tourist families. The supposed outlaw hippies of the past hiding in the hills unaware of the hell brewing below.

It took ten minutes for the supermarket to chase me away , of course due to some redneck unable to bear the sight of a person smiling and speaking to strangers. So I meet up with another of our horde and we start juggling outside the McDonalds accross the way. just as things are getting good and people are beeing cheered out of their dreadful lives along comes mister nasty cop at the service of goody-two red shoes Ronald McDeathhold. We politely agree to terminate our utterly outrageous behavior because we were "... bothering the customers". But, ohhh noo that's not good enough for the fucking godsucking piece'o shit pig, he's gotta ask our names as if we should have them pinned to our shirts like him. Well it's none your fuckin busyness who I am, I think rambling off an a.k.a. claiming to have no I.D. My attitude changed abruptly however when he ordered us to his car for a scenic trip to jail where we were to stay until he was sure we weren't "running from the law "

So I had no good reason to hide my identity, I didn't have any warrants, I guess I didn't want to go through the hassle of explaining why I, a Canadian was broke and begging in the deep south. On top of that , usually when a cop has taken my name down on a slip of paper and left.
That wasn't the case, my comrade and I were wisked off to the station. I proceeded in building a huge false identity to answer his questions with. All the details; social security number , place of birth , parents names ,diplomas ect. hoping he'd give up.
This was another mistake ,for this particular pig was set on busting someone. He was driving us around town looking for my van or someone to ID us , for some reason I thought someone from our group would be able to guess my lies. NO luck the one person we did encounter didn't even know my real name. figureing they'd search me I eventually caved in showed them my I.D. and explained that I had been lying , this was difficult to do but I felt I had no choice. I even told him I'd been caught off guard when asked my name. He was not understanding in the least. The guy with me got out shortly after coming clean, he hadn't lied, much.

Big thanks to ANGIE for sending this piece from Cana"duh"
There's a better version sitting on the hard drive of a broken computer at C-Squat, alas.

Some of our gang showed up afterwards, I got a glance of them asking about the situation and heard that I would likely be freed. The officer in charge off the case came in the cell now and again as if just to frighten me with questions and scold me for breaking the law. Then the door swayed open and I was beckoned out, my knife was returned and I was sat down to answer some final questions . With relief I began laying down the truth. All seemed fine then then the guy asks my home address.

Doing my best to tell the truth , "I don't really have a home sir so I'll give you my...."

"That's it, I'm charging you " he says gesturing for me to return the knife. That was it amidst talk of deportation I was scuttled off to the car. It was around this point I decided to ask why he hadn't read my rights.

"It's not required anymore." the response. I told him I was going to stop talking and nothing more was said until I reached the county jail.

The county jail was much larger and more heavily staffed, and way more serious. They didn't make any jokes or off color comments nothing, they were stern even towards the town cop who quickly filled out a report and left me in their hands. They had already printed me and taken my mug shots when my girlfriend and another of our horde arrived,looking more woried than I did ,but inside I was surely under more stress. I asked when I would see a lawyer.

"A few days before your court appearance on the 18th",one the grim pigs grunted.

"Ahh! only a few weeks", I said to the window where my two friends were climbing over one another to see me for maybe the last time for a while.

"That's the 18th of August", he said.

"Two & half months" I gulped , as my girlfriends expresion sunk. I tried calling my mother with my one phonecall,... busy.

"Call my mother !! ",I shouted as I was pushed along the way out of my last sight of my weeping lover , for at least two long months,only next of kin were allowed visting priveledges.Bail , well I was sure it'd be to much for anyone to come up with fast.

At this point I was far to apprehensive of what was to come next to think about how stupid this whole thing was. In reality I had done nothing wrong ,who is harmed by my standing to the side of their path juggling and asking for donations, and what right do police have to see my identification ,when I'm truly not causing harm. THe laws used against me were definately being abused, to cleanse the community of undesireables who might harm their spic'n span tourist town image.

I didn't mind too much when they took everything I owned away from me and made me dress in foolish looking orange clothes with cheap rubber lipflops. It was only mildly humiliating to shower while an ugly redneck watches from the halway holding his billy club ,intimidating but short lived . So what ,he barks at me to pick up my bed roll, you feel vunerable everytime you turn your back to them ,let alone bending over. The walk to my cell was what I feared , all the hecklers ,getting spit at, meeting your new boyfriends . Nothing though, they were all locked up.In my cell ,slam and there I am.

...mate of course wakes to greet me, luckily he's no threat not even a real criminal ,in jail for failure to pay a fine.He even gave me an apple.We exchanged a few stories then he rambled on about how it used to be a great place, Eureka Springs , now the police were even after any local who looked a bit off white.When he returned to sleep I surveyed my surroundings half expecting to find a way out, then lay restlessly in bed shocked ."how the fuck did I end up here?". With nothing to do in that box I drifted off to sleep dreading meeting my neighbors in the morning.

I awoke to the sound of an explosion , looking over at my cellmate,still asleep, I jumped to the door. Peering through smoke I saw nothing but heard screams and gunshots. This worried me and I looked about futilely for a way out again nothing.Looking again through the tiny window I watched as a pig fell to the ground squeeling blood spurting on the glass, then to my joy out of the smoke jumped Psychokitty AK in hand followed closely by lizard boy squeezing off a few more rounds down the hallway out of my sight.

I banged on the door ,"Over here, quick let me out , hey!! Over here!!" the beautiful heroine leaped over the roast pork keys out and ready to free me.

"Fast, Fast!!", I shouted ,anxious to escape ,as I saw lizard boy shake of and knock out another swine who'd jumped on him from a side room.

Loud as could be the bolt slid "shhlunk",I jumped to attention only to face one of the same old grim goully pigheaded incarcerating motherfuckers gesturing for me to "roll that shit up and follow me."I'm led to the room were I had left my clothes an told to change back.

"You remember that nigger,Jimmy , the one down the valley who..."

" He weren't no niger Charlie ,he's alright liked baseball and everything."

"Guess you're right, hurry up in there!"

I had paused to listen, not much ,but I wasn't surprised when I found out later that the chief at that station had been a high ranking member in the klan.They returned my things and told me to show up for my court date or I'd have a warrant for failure to appear, however they wouldn't extradite if I wasn't caught in Arkansas. I had nothing to say but goodbye, as left the building to find Psychokitty & Lizard Boy waiting for me with beer in the Black Box. By morning we were all in Oklahoma on our way to Austin.

Bail had been set at $300.00 . In effect my mother had just payed that money to get me out of jail and I was told not to return to Arkansas .

I don't intend to!

I used to be afraid of traveling in the deep south. People are always coming up with police horror stories and sweet strains of squeel like pig".Finally though we put fear aside and do what we ucking please , well don't you? Whatever ,One need only be aware f the differences in the south and with a bit of caution it's not oo dangerous. Two suggestions (1) If you have a warrent on your ead,have a solid A.K.A. and don't carry I.D. . (2) And ,if you do arry I.D. don't bother to give a false name .

P.S.   It's also nice to have someone somewhere who'll bail you out
       Thanx Mom .... Thanx Martine

So I'm gonna pass the narration along to Comrade Balaam for minute while I get some papers in order for the next chapter. This is one of the flyers that was floating around that wee Austin. I'm pretty sure it was drawn by Nimby of the Phuckharwee Tribe (Phuckharwee as in Where the Phuckharwee?

a *Warehouse Productions* and THE NOMADIC CIRCUS
Present

July 6th
Blort
Brown Hornet
23 Aliens

July 7th
Red Scare
99 Pounds
Primitive Echo
Circus ov All Saints

WISH YOU WERE HERE

July 8th
Cactus Smack
Cornpone
Coprolingus

July 9th
Phuck Harwee
Blister Fetish
Fairy Stain
Latex Chicken

PHASE
PHOLKS
GET IN
PHREE
(ASK OSCAR)

A GATHERING OF THE TRIBES

Fire Eaters   *Smart Bar (no stupid bar)*
Tattoo Artists   *Body Piercing*
Jewelry   *DJ Interludes*
Bondage Show   *Fireside Chats*

$5 ONLY
PER
NIGHT

JULY 6-9 , 1995

FOR FURTHER INFO CALL   (512) 385·6856
or 385·6786

Balaam's Tale:

So here is my account of the events shortly before and shortly after my involvement with the Nomadic Festival. My name is Balaam. I'm an American squatter from the North-Eastern metropolis, mostly from Philly, PA. I've squatted the east coast block for a huge chunk of my life. I've made music, started dinky labels, put out zines, and helped open squats. Never content to just sit, spange for beer, and sell my soul to habitual drugs; and not quite satisfied with the up & down-in&out semi-scene Philly had for music (suburban teenagers thinking they could change the world through hardcore); I fled.

Joining a thousand rats on a treadmill HEADING west, bound for the Rockies or the Bay Area or anywhere but Philly. I traveled here and there and anywhere the tracks or my thumb could take me, left people in places, picked people up in places, and carried my mobile home on my back for an eternity. Until one day I fell into a spider web within the borders of Louisiana. Eviction! New address: Orleans Parish Prison, Building CCC, one of the seven jails that helped to carry the New Orleans economy. Now, seven of us made the mistake of squatting in the French Quarter. Three of us were extradited to our home towns and four of us were said to have been released two days later. One of us was not. So I rotted in jail for seventy days until my folks, who I hadn't spoken to since Philly (Hello Dad- I'm in jail!) convinced the warden to let me go.

Needless to say, while i was on ice I did a lot of thinking. I came to the conclusion that now i had seen most of the country and had been primarily unproductive, I was going to stay put for a while and attempt to stir shit up. One of the first people I had met after being released was Sascha. Sascha is a New York squatter who, if I encountered him earlier I might not have left the East Coast. He and his friends from the Nomadic Festival are phenomenal networkers and kick ass statement-makers and far from what I was used to seeing from the East Coast. They definitely changed my opinion of the Lower East Side.

When I first met Sascha I didn't read too much into what he told me. He gave me a copy of Arrow's Nom Fest recruiting flier. I read the patch and was pleasantly surprised to relate to someone else's lofty goals but I didn't expect much. Looking back I regret not getting involved sooner. At first glance I was mainly inspired by Sascha's energy. He's a purple heart Kinko's veteran known for his cynical patches and sticker designs. Shortly after Mardi Gras I left for Austin.

With Arrow's flier in my pocket I ran into Sascha again at a Crash Worship show. He left Austin after a week or two, but in that time i ran into so many options I couldn't leave with him and I knew that this was a good place to fuck shit up.

I found myself in the middle of a squatter crisis in town. The Austin Chronicle published a derogatory article about our lifestyle which resulted in changes. Local stores that had once accepted food stamps stopped, the police did an intense sweeping of the streets and arrested people for lack of I.D.'s lack of minimal pocket cash, dogs were impounded for lack of papers, the only existing squat at the time was evicted and two outdoor camps were raided. So I got a notebook and collected as many letters to the editor as I could (about 15) and sent the letters to the Chronicle. They were published and many more letters after that were published for and against our response. This was just the kind of volatile atmosphere I needed to stay put in and keep from rotting.

I began living in a warehouse squat which turned commune, then turned underground hang out/ club. Then it turned ugly. The guy who got the lease for the place saw what we were capable of and developed a messiah complex. He was a discharged army drone–ex-Baptist-absentee father turned rainbow hippy who was amazed with our involvement with Food Not Bombs, was impressed with the achievements of the former Chaos Collective that used to drive the warehouse, and thought it necessary to wrench our plans for the future by appointing himself leader/ minister and painted the letters C.H.U.R.CH. on the front of the warehouse. He then consecutively pissed off every connection we had in town and turned off everyone we had recruited to be involved in the project of starting a temporary autonomous zone or a close facsimile thereof.

Suddenly the phone rings... After three months I'm hearing Sascha's voice again. It's exciting how powerful our network is that, after two brief periods with Sascha in my life and three without, this kid knows my number, address, resources, and pattern of bowel movements. That was enough to forget about my current situation. "Sure I'll help you with the Nom Fest! Send me your shit and I'll see what I can do!" As soon as he hangs up- BOOM- I'm looking at the second coming of Jim Jones. Nevertheless I was still excited that Sascha and Arrow were sticking to their guns, so I made some plans and phone calls and got some takers for the idea. I called Arrow and told him the outlined master plan for Austin about a week after Sascha's call.

This turned out to be all in vein as life on the homefront had gotten worse, and I was forced to abandon the plan. Our "messiah" had taken to stealing our belongings, spending house funds, altering our records, and claiming that our little treasury had been robbed by a mysterious stranger and that he had been kicked down a glorious motorcycle by an imaginary friend all in the same breath. I hadn't forgotten about the Festival but it was after their starting date and I hadn't heard from anybody. After the Philly date I called some friends and was told that the Nomadic Festival fell apart and that nothing happened in Philly, so I focused my attention on going over our house ledger with a fine toothed comb with Greg, our house genius.

It didn't take long to get everybody to recognize the magnitude of our problem and soon the lynch mob was after Father Dickhead. "Why was he such a problem?" you ask, "Why didn't we just oust the motherfucker?" Well, this place has had such a long history. It's functioned as a squat for years. People had come and gone, shows were put on, scenes were started and re-started and there were very few external threats. Two people even died there twice upon a time and the place didn't get shut down. But along comes our hero who reminds the owners of the building that they should be making money off this place and manages to etch his solitary name, with the movie star glitz of his stately military background, to a lease which would give him legal sovereignty over all the peon streetpeople dwelling illegally in the building.

RRRRIIINNGG....It's Sascha again. "Oh yeah, things are going pretty well. They started off kind of rocky, but we should be there close to schedule. How are things there?" So the second off the phone, I got right back on again. I had been to anarchist gatherings, rainbow fiascoes, and had enough traveling under my belt to know what to shoot for, but at this point I had wasted enough time. I was hearing stories of parades and parties and this that and the other object. So with some two weeks to get shit together, I went for what was easiest. We had been a factory for Crash Worship's Drum Quest show just before things went awry. So with those kinds of connections, and Austin's unique music scene, it made sense to put together a Crash-Worshipesque tribal music festival.

I made a bunch of phone calls and started to work out the details. With a lot of initial success, my friends and housemates took interest, soon became psyched, and together we rapidly became the smoothest production company. We managed to get bands, technicians, footsoldiers, and riot starters interested in the first week. The miracle was that anyone would subject themselves to such a short notice, low budget headache. with only the promise of "we don't know how many people will come, but it should be fun." These weren't just obscure garage bands, mind you. The lighting and sound technicians were from some of Austin's prominent productions in the live music capital of the world, and we had some of Austin's best bands, weird as they may be. So it was mildly exciting at first.

Then as we spent the final week promoting this monstrosity, our domestic problems fired up again. The Fucker threatened to call it off, then considered it a good business opportunity, then kicked me out. When the Nomads whom I'd developed a lot of respect for arrived, the real fireworks started. I was trying to ignore my eviction threats, trying to put the finishing touches to our two-week-old leap of faith, trying ever so hard to ignore the little fling that one of the nomads was having with my fiancee, trying to end a fling-turned- Fatal Attraction-soap opera which seemed to be further ruining my ruined sanity. Then, just as things were going so peachy, his holy venerable assholeness decided to begin kicking out the people we had been working our asses off to bring in. So by the time we reached the starting gate, we had some catching up to do.

Amazingly enough, we had managed to pull in a decent crowd for the first night of our four day trip. Then we ran into technical difficulties. We got over that hurtle though and soon it was day two. Now the bastard was working the shit out of the Nom Fest crew, having them do everything short of brushing his teeth and wiping his ass. My status was shaky at this point. I was still attempting to smooth rough edges with that night's show. I was begging my Nom Fest friends not to pay attention to fuckhead and trying to entertain them with the finer points of Austin. Then it was back to Kinko's to make more fliers to try to pull in a larger crowd for that night.. I was trying not to pay too much attention to the fact that I was in that night's headlining band, and trying to remind myself that when I had first met my current girlfriend she had a boyfriend who she was cheating on with me and that we were both honest now and had an open relationship and that it was perfectly normal that I walked in on her last night with him and that it was all just because I was really busy right now and couldn't spend much time with her and there's nothing wrong with me and FUCK I GO ON IN ONE MINUTE!! I guess I'd better get back to the warehouse.

Holy shit, that night looked fucking amazing. Everyone was either breathing fire, twirling torches, drumming, or writhing naked in front of an enormous crowd for what was expected. The band I was in had only played together twice before: once on the radio and once on a public access TV show. The show went on and on metamorphosing into a baptism of fire and drum circles which kept their energy until the cops turned it off. The lights went on and the people cleared out.. My love came up to me, "He wants to go for a ride with me." ("You don't mind, do ya? Love ya buh bye."

Only two casualties and one death occurred. One drunken frat fuck decided he knew how to breathe fire and burned his face off. Then the next day news came in that there was a car accident and one kid was killed, another in intensive care, and a girl who walked away with severe mental scars. We found out that day that the driver of the car was drunk and expected to stay at the gathering, as he was told he could but had been asked to leave by, you guessed it, the great messiah himself. I couldn't think straight at this point From the interior the Nom Fest and all of my friends saw the fiasco that was taking place but the show went on out of respect for those who were giving up their time. From the exterior the people were still getting a good show and they were even buying books and being exposed to the Nomadic Festivals anarchist literature. As for me everybody inside and out was seeing a stressed out joke who could hardly organize his life, let alone an autonomous gathering.

The show that night was another good display but the energy was angry. Afterwards I saw a gathering of squatters conducting what could only be described as a wake.. Later on, while trying to sleep in my room, Sascha witnessed what was the worst nervous breakdown and most intense signal my brain has ever sent me. The next and last day of the Austin fest the nomads packed up to leave, then decided to have a meeting whether or not to abandon the last day of the gathering. So "fuck it" I said as I did the only logical thing I could think of doing. I disappeared until the Nom Fest was about to pull away.

Two days later I was homeless and fried. Where would I rather be than with my friends, who were probably laughing at me at this point. I called up the next stop where the nomads would be and caught up with them in time to enjoy what for me was a extremely good vacation.. I saw a beautiful example of a successful autonomist gathering, a reunion with two of my best friends, a healing time for my girlfriend and me, and the chance to be part of an impressive passive demonstration in the streets of Berkeley as the Nomadic Festival triumphantly, chaotically, yet beautifully united with the anarchists of Berkeley, parading and blocking many of the major roads.

Looking forward to next year...   Balaam

WORD ON THE STREETS HAS IT THAT BALAAM + LIZ ARE HOMELESS AGAIN - SO THIS ADDRESS IS PROBABLY USELESS. IF YOU WANT TO TRACK THEM DOWN CONTACT PROJECT PHASE IN AUSTIN.

WE ARE THE 801ST GENERATION OF HOMOSAPIENS TO WALK THE EARTH. FOR MUCH OF OUR HISTORY THE PRIMARY DESIRE OF THE SPECIES HAS BEEN FOR MATERIAL SECURITY AT ANY COST. THE 800TH GENERATION CAME DANGEROUSLY CLOSE TO SATISFYING THIS WISH. WE NOW HAVE TO CHANGE WHAT WE DESIRE BEFORE OUR OWN SUCCESS KILLS US. THE 801ST GENERATION WAS BORN KNOWING CHANGE IS THE ONLY CONSTANT. WE OUR OURSELVES THE EMBODYMENT OF CHANGE. WE CHANGE LOCATION, APPEARANCE, AND EVEN PERSONALITY AS NATURALLY AS THE SEASONS SHIFT OR THE MOON MOVES INTO A NEW PHASE. WE KNOW INSTINCTIVLY THAT CHANGE IS AN ACT OF CREATION, CREATION AN ACT OF DESTRUCTION. WE KNOW THAT THE WHOLE IS GREATER THAN THE SUM OF ITS PARTS, AND THAT EACH PART CONTAINS THE WHOLE. WE RUMMAGE THROUGH THE OLD WAYS AND PICK OUT THE BEST BITS, LEARN WHAT WE CAN, WHERE WE CAN, AND LEAVE ALONE WHAT WE DO NOT NEED. WE MAKE WHAT WE CANNOT FIND AND CREATE WHAT WE THINK SHOULD EXIST. WE LAUGH AT ATTEMPTS TO STICK US IN CATEGORIES. WHY APPLY A LABEL TODAY? WE WILL BE SOMETHING ELSE TOMORROW. MUSIC IS WHAT DEFINES US TO OURSELVES. MUSIC IS THE FLUID LANGUAGE WE USE TO SPEAK TO EACH OTHER, TO EXPRESS THE PERSPECTIVES FROM WHICH WE SEE THE WORLD. WE SIGH, WE SCREAM, WE SEND OUT A PULSING BEAT. THE STOMPING OF OUR FEET MAKES THE PLANET RATTLE. MUSIC CONNECTS US TO ONE ANOTHER. MUSIC IS A PALPABLE LINK TO THE PAST. ON A CRESTING WAVE OF MUSIC WE RIDE TODAY INTO THE FUTURE. WE ARE THE 801ST GENERATION OF HOMO SAPIENS TO WALK THE EARTH. DANCING WITH OUR ANCESTORS, SINGING TO OUR CHILDREN, WE ARE THE LIVING BREATH OF CONTINOUS EVOLUTION.

GATHERING OF THE TRIBES

THE 801ST GENERATION   BY DAVE.

The Patch

There's this feeling you might get sometimes that you're part of something much bigger and greater than yourself. I'm not talking about a higher power making decisions about your life for you, I'm talking about something that's partly your creation, that you have a role in building. I'm talking about connections and people and life in the underground. The feeling's not something you have to define with words but it's something you know is a part of you and will be a part of you wherever you travel and whatever situations you find yourself in. It's not necessary something you claim allegiance to, like a soldier would fight for a country - I'm talking about an unspoken bond between people - a code that changes form and face through time and however you mold it yourself, but has the same core - is rooted in something timeless. Sometimes you can feel it when you're with a bunch of your friends - a big group working together on big things. Sometimes you catch glimpses of it in small things, what might be just a funny coincidence but you know it can't be. That's when the feeling hits and you remember.

One night during the Austin leg of the festival I ended up talking to this trainhopper kid Jeff who I'd never met before. Jeff was from Olympia, Washington and had been on the road for a while and was decked out in the nearly universal traveling punk uniform - boots, black encrusted and sown up jeans, black denim jacket covered in spikes and patches, face piercings, dirty dreadlocks. I have kind of this habit of checking out the patches on traveling punks' attire cause in the past few years anarchist groups and bands from all over the place have been printing and distributing patches and you start to see the same ones after a while. If you have an eye for it and you're pretty up on the different scenes around the country, it's pretty easy to tell where people have been or where they're from by the patches on their clothes. It's a whole little underworld of symbols and hidden meanings really only meant for a small group of people.

It might seem uninteresting to most and for good reason, but I have this funny history with patches that started when I was fourteen and coming of age in the punk scene in New York. Back then there was this woman who sang for one of the local anarchist squatter bands who I was totally in awe of and respected almost to the point of worship and one day this woman gave me a silkscreened canvas patch with her band's logo on it that I'd only ever seen people in her band wearing. These were the days before patches were all over the place and everyone was making and distributing them, so it was a big deal to an impressionable kid like me. I sowed it in a prominent place on my punked out jacket and wore it proudly until it faded and eventually got so dirty it was unreadable. It was a powerful thing, that patch, because it meant I was hooked into the scene I'd only watched from afar, and it made me feel like I was a part of something real for the first time in my life.

Anyway, that memory stuck with me and when I was sixteen I took a high school printmaking class and cut out my first silkscreen. It was a simple two color rectangular design - the black and red Anarcho-syndiclist flag from the Spanish Civil War with the silhouette of a figure holding a rifle in the background. My art teacher, Mr. Leventhal, told me it was a good example of crude talentless propaganda and I'd be better off making linoleum blocks of cows because they had more soul. Nonetheless, I was really proud of it and found a strip of painting canvas in the back of the room and cut it up into little rectangular pieces to make my first patch. I printed about fifteen of them before the screen died and I gave them out to a bunch of my friends. I figured if I could give something to people around me that would inspire them nearly as much as that patch the woman had given to me I couple years earlier, it would be totally worth it.

Skipping over a lot of time, about four years later I was playing in a punk rock band myself and practicing at C-squat, playing shows around the neighborhood and getting ready to do a small tour in Canada. We decided we wanted to print up a bunch of patches and shirts for the tour, so my friend who silkscreened for a living and had a whole shop out in Brooklyn, hooked us up with his light table and taught a

KILL YOUR TELEVISION

couple of us how to do it. We ended up stealing a whole lot of ink from a big art supply store in the city and dumpstering a bunch of shirts and the whole thing cost us next to nothing. It was cool because we could print right outside our shows, straight on to people's clothes for free and it was a good way of getting our name around and also showing people that silkscreening was really easy and didn't have to cost a lot of money.

Around the same time I got really into printing patches and made up a whole bunch of screens with different people's artwork and went around giving out patches all the time to my friends. I liked the feeling that I was printing this underground currency that had no value in the outside world, but was priceless in the circuits I traveled. Cutting up rolls of canvas into pieces and reproducing these powerful symbols, giving and exchanging gifts without the use of money. Not ever being too good with my hands or feeling like I was very artistic, it was the first time I was ever making something concrete and solid and it felt good to see people all over the place wearing stuff I made.

Eventually I really needed money and I started selling them on the street for dollar and actually financed a journey across the country almost entirely from that money, showing up in towns and laying out my goods in the main square. I'd always end up giving away a bunch of patches to cool people I met, but surprisingly I got pretty good at selling them to almost anyone from frat boys to old ladies. Taking something from our scene and marketing it seemed pretty sketchy to me, but it was really small time on the street and we're not talking about something with mass appeal anyway, just a handy means of survival for a traveling guy such as myself. Anyway, that's my story with the patches.

So with that all out of the way, we're back at the Church in Austin last summer and I'm talking to Jeff the trainhopper kid and checking out the patches on his jacket cause there are a bunch I've never seen before. One of them strikes my eye because it's two colored and I move closer to get a better look at it. Suddenly I'm thrown into this state of amazement and disbelief and I get even closer to make sure I'm right. Usually when I meet someone who's wearing one of my patches it's a cool little reminder of how tight-knit our scene is, but this was too strange.

"Where...where did you get that?" I manage to get out of my stunned mouth because I know I'm right but it doesn't make any sense. "Oh, that. I traded it with this girl I was traveling with from the East coast, but I don't know where she got it from. I think it's really old." We never even figured out how it happened or where the connection was and in the end it didn't really matter because the whole thing was so beautiful and mysterious we didn't need to know. Here I was in Austin, Texas - talking to a guy from Olympia, Washington who somehow ended up wearing one of the fifteen old Anarcho-Syndiclist patches I printed when I was sixteen years old in New York.

I was delirious from sleep and pot, not enough of the former and way too much of the latter, uncharacteristically stoned for the first time in months; my mind moving as if in slow motion like waves of molasses or road heat mirages. I was standing at the top of an old windmill on a piece of farmland outside Clovis New Mexico, a few miles South of Interstate 40. The sun was just beginning to blaze from its pearch at the top of the sky, the air was hot and dry and I couldn't help thinking about all the chalk white bones I'd seen by the side of the road in my previous visits to the desert - bleached white by the sun's rays. My head was swimming in the enormity of it all, thinking about the far away ocean by the coast and imaginary pieces of blue beach glass smooth and rounded after years of being shaped by the surf; the ways the sea and the desert are the same, how they can ground the strongest things down till they're no more than dust or sand. How you don't fuck with them if you're smart.

I could see the horizon streching out in every direction, the land flat for miles everywhere, nothing but dry land and our crew milling restlessly below. We had left Austin in a hurry only a day before, our numbers swelled to three vehicle capacity and our hearts anxious to find some peace in the desert after a hectic week in Texas. Although there had been a lot of new people around and some really talented and dedicated folks, the gathering at The Church had been somewhat of a disaster - infighting and messy coordination and power hungry messiah-types and stuff like that.

OVERLOOKING THE RIO GRANDE IN TAOS, NM

But we had a bunch of cool new people who'd joined our ranks. Megan from Philadelphia had hopped trains from the Food Not Bombs gathering in San Francisco and finally hooked up with us in Austin. Sara and Harry, hobo couple extrodinare, lured by promises of adventure and glory, scrapped their plans to settle down and joined up with us. Loki, who'd hung with us for a little while in Atlanta and had made it all the way to Barstow California on the rails, was sitting in a trainyard when he decided he'd come back and meet up with us in Austin. Trevor, Road Warrior from Raligh North Carolina with a heart of gold and a ton of hand crafted armor adorning his body, jumped on the wagon.

The original crew had planned this renesvous with the Atlanta folks weeks before and now that we were here it was obvious it wasn't where we were supposed to be - a desolate piece of land with nothing growing on it except our frustration and a bunch of weeds. With no plans and a bunch of differing opinions, the Nomadic Festival had kind of degenerated into a bunch of bickering sleepless kids.

Staring out into the distance, looking down at our temporary host's makeshift shelter, a rundown camper trailer with plastic tarps suspended by poles surrounding the outside, I wondered to myself how I had ended up in this crazy situation. I say I, not we, because I had a very strange sensation of being disconnected from everyone below me. Smoking pot always makes me super-introverted and quiet, and all of a sudden I became really conscious of my**self**, and everybody else's **self**, and I could feel all our conflicting **selfs**, scattering like a dust cloud but stuck together through circumstance in this vast wasteland.

So eventually we had a plan going on and we said goodbye to the Atlanta crew with plans to meet up that Friday in the main square in Santa Fe. Our posse caravaned to Taos where we camped for a couple nights by the Rio Grande and bathed in hot springs and slept under the blue moon. But before we got there some funny stuf happened to us along the way.

This is a story about what happened one day when we were all sitting in a parking lot of some supermarket in New Mexico:

Danny (known for his Great Tact) borrowed Chuck's megaphone and started spewing a barrage of profanities and insults directed at the manager of the supermarket for reasons still unbeknownst to us. It was blisteringly hot outside and we were on our way to find some body of water we could all soak our sweaty skins in. Just as we were about to pull out and continue on our quest, the police showed up and detained us for questioning. They took identification from all of us (except for Loki whose record was riddled with warrants - he was cowering in the back of Black Box with the dogs.) What was so funny was that here we were, a big crew of people traveling together, and we all had ID from different places. The cops were checking records from Ohio, Louisiana, New York, Oregon, North Carolina, Washington, Nova Scotia, Pennsylvania, California, Virginia, Ontario, Minnesota, Colorado, you name it, we had someone from there with us. After not being able to find the suspected megaphone, they finally asked us what we were doing all traveling together. It was a good question. We didn't really have an answer AT the time. They finally let us go.

Corvus Corax

NOMADIC FESTIVAL

FRIDAY JULY 14th AT THE CCA / WAREHOUSE 1614 PASEO DE PERALTA

When we all met up that Friday in Santa Fe, the Corvus Corax clan, a group of old traveling friends, invited us to perform with them at some warehouse that night. It was total chaos. There were four bands that played: a weird kind of jazz experimental band, a riot girl band, a pop punk/hardcore type band, and Corvus Corax, basically a slow, grinding, death-metal band. The crowd was pretty confused. We were outside doing our fire and drum jam and the security people were freaking out. Drunk mayhem. When it was all over, an eight vechicle caravan (including the Corvus huge black schoolbus) made its way out to Diablo Canyon where we all pretty much collapsed from exhaustion.

Somehow we ended up in Albequerque to see a Los Crudos show (great punk band from Chicago) a couple days later. Fred's Bagels (remember this if you're ever in Albequerque) gives away free meals to members of touring bands and we somehow managed to convince them that all fifteen of us were in the rock extravaganza "Carnival of Chaos" and they showered us in sandwiches and soup and coffee. We stayed to watch the show at some punk house that day and I remember feeling really protective of our crew, really tight with everyone on foreign territory.

CONGRADULATIONS: YOU'VE REACHED THE CENTER OF "CARNIVAL OF CHAOS: ON THE ROAD WITH THE NOMADIC FESTIVAL SUMMER '95: THIS IS TOTAL FILLER.

X   Compatriots in beleaguering distances, upon receiving tidings I in good spirits lift thy horn. Hail!

We as a might of fellowship in this cantankerous clime are indeed honing our skills and painstakingly trudging through emotional "quagmires". The junction we are to pass, A blessing all to prophesied. For this event you are conjuring, is something we are in our own accord undoubtedly going to execute.

Though still shrouded, our route is to go down southwest, up the west coast, cantering to Canada and stresslessly head east. In this migration a possible descension to particular locations in the Mid-west, cutting back up to Canada and blazing the final trail to the east-coast. Where we will be hoarding gold to say the last of our riddances so to feast on the exploits abroad. This is open to change to comply with your company, for the garrison amassed shall be the bane of all.

We have now in the form of mobility, a bus and steadily is our equipment gaining with only a few items to obtain, this including a cleverly contrived metal percussion unit. Unfortunately, we will not have a demo for another month or so, but have a boonful resource of doing the recording for free by an associate of a band entitled "Deadworld".

There is yet so much to relay, for excitement comith in the horizened tomorrows, but what is the need to say when life itself will be fulfilled by the awe of this gathering destiny. A spirituality transcending nebulously the limit of words and it is this that exhumes the true bond of brotherly allegiance. My good neighboring tribesmen, soon indeed shall we cheer to the coming raze. Lord Malus Stormcrow and all of the Corvus Coven.

So we did the long haul through the desert from Albequerque to Oakland - straight shot Interstate 40 to Interstate 5 with almost everyone tweaking on crystal meth procured from one of Arrow's old high school buddies - it was a crazy ride. We only stopped for gas and cigarettes the whole way. Everyone who wasn't speeding was tripping from sleep deprivation - screaming at each other back and forth on the CB's and blasting the music.

After a week of exploring in the desert, we were all of a sudden thrown back into the schedule we had created for ourselves, racing against time to get to

the Bay Area before the Born of Fire gathering began. We had been traveling this way for a month and a half, not settling down anywhere for more than a couple days, throwing ourselves into orbit so that it started to seem natural after a while to get back on the road just as we had arrived somewhere. This wasn't the first time during the Summer that I started thinking it was a little ridiculous that we were moving so fast with so little purpose except to *get there*. The best part about traveling is that freedom to end up wherever fate takes you, no worries about time or where you're supposed to be. But we knew exactly where we were supposed to be and we were very much on time. We were also spending every last penny on gas.

I remember stopping at some gas station in the middle of the night when Black Box was almost running on empty and the gas was $1.50 a gallon. "That's outrageous!" I deliriously screamed at the gas attendant guy. He then informed me with a smile that there was some rich fuck who owned every gas station within sixty miles and the price wasn't going to change until we left the area of his monopoly. Oh.

I remember watching the sunrise outside Flagstaff, Arizona and then me and Megan trying to sleep in the back of Black Box with Blue Dog as Martine and Pete blasted some hip-hop tape and the van started to cook in the desert sun.

I remember thinking we were going to show up at the Born of Fire gathering just in time and then sleep for two days.

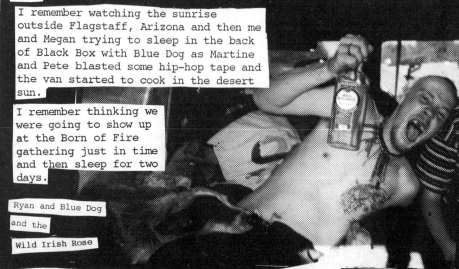

Ryan and Blue Dog
and the
Wild Irish Rose

BORN OF FIRE

A GATHERING OF HERETICS & LUNATICS, AUTONOMISTS & TRIBALISTS.
JULY 18-22, 1995
SAN FRANCISCO BAY AREA

A five day respite from the banal mediocrity of daily life. A revolt against domestication. A temporary autonomous zone. Deviants of all stripes will be coming together for a few days to live and play outside of the spectacle society and it's various systems of oppression- work, school, church, state, to name a few. So come join us if you want to smash some TVs, make some music, learn a new skill, and maybe even disrupt business as usual for a moment

anger/play/words/action/art/music/love

info: 3833 clarke st., oakland, ca 94609 ph: 510.601.7476 or 510.597.0469

The Bay Area - Oakland, Berkeley, San Francisco - is the radical mecca of North America (at least it felt like it after traveling through the South for so long.) It's a strange pocket of resistance that attracts freaks from all walks of life. The original paths carved in the 60's, the whole area has a rich history of radical politics and crazy wacked out shit.

But the state of California itself has one of the most repressive, backward, racist governments in the country and the small amount of revolutionary groups in the Bay or hippie communes in the woods are far outnumbered on all sides by conservative suburban homes, hellish cities like Los Angeles, and old retired military people and huges bases in the desert further South. It's a strange place - as beautiful and sunny as it is, California always seems to be getting hit by crazy plague like, biblical disasters - forest fires, floods, earth quakes. Everybody seems to think it's eventually all going to fall in the ocean.

Dear Arrow,

I was thinking it would be great to have a conference thing where the majority of workshops provided an opportunity to learn/teach a skill, or make something, or go somewhere, or get concrete information about the inspiring activities of others...When I read about what you had in mind it gave me the determination to plunge forward because the two projects seem very symbiotic in nature and, if scheduled to coincide, could benefit one another; Your entourage could have a ready made, exciting "event", and an easy way to meet local punks/activists, and the Oakland festival would have rad additional participants with exotic non-regional perspectives. I've started organizing loosely and so when I know for sure when the Nom. Fest. wagons roll into town(now ed.) I can start having some serious meetings. I have tons of ideas for workshops. A few definates and hopefuls are: self defence, bike repair, a mud people fiesta in the financial district, a writing workshop, stencil making (with midnight stenciling expedition to follow), herbal medicine 101, wilderness/urban survival info exchange, scams-shoplifting and sabotage, pirate radio (maybe an actual gathering-orienting radio could occur), sign and puppet making (perhaps an anticonsumerist death machine public event at the end of the week to utilize the fruits of this workshop?),

a couple of urban exploration field trip options, a tv smashing party, drum circles, and whatever empowering and productive agenda items manifest during the coming months.

I'm figuring this extravaganza could span four days and have a fifth-day picnic free-for-all at the park. I'm hoping the workshops can all be at one location, but I also hope local collective spaces will want to join the fun. I'm thinking of night time shows, performances, video viewings, etc., at Epicenter Zone, Gilman St., and the Long Hall.

I would to here from anyone with input, ideas, or advice. In a couple of months(a month now. ed.) people can request more detailed/

logistical info on this event if they like. Another thing is I'll try to compile a list of possible places to crash and set up a phone tree for couch and floor accommodations during the week of the event. So people can certainly contact me about that.

Your Nom. Fest. sounds absolutely great and I'll be happy if it really happens. I'm totally looking forward to meeting wonderful people and basking in the togetherness and demarginalization. "A symphony of souls is the sort of thing everyone's lives seem to need right now. It will be a great summer if everything goes well.—Matty V.H. 3833 Clark St.,

Oakland, CA 94609 (510)601-7476.

There's this weird split between the East Bay (Oakland/Berkele
and the West Bay (San Francisco) scenes which is hard to
understand until you spend a bunch of time in both places.
Usually people choose one or the other to claim affiliation to
I'm no exception.
People living in SF talk a lot of shit about the East Bay - bu
I love it. Food Not Bombs is always serving at People's Park,
there are punk houses all over the place, pirate radio station
creeping up out of the cracks in the system, underground tunnel
to play in, the Longhaul Infoshop, abandoned chemical factorie
to explore by the water, the Berkeley hills, a ton of left ove
acid casuality wingnuts walking around the streets, probably a
dozen libraries you can sneak into on the campus and read unti
you can't see straight, you know, the simple things in life.

The week of the gathering was a time for us to meet up with old
friends, go to the workshops at Gilman St. and Golden Gate
Park, parade around in a big mass. For the first time all
summer we didn't have to do anything - everything was already
set up. By the time we made it there, it seemed like we had
destroyed and recreated ourselves seven or eight times over
already. People coming and going - bringing new energy from
each place we stopped - taking it with us to the next place -
pushing us along, knocking us back. We never really had built
up the momentum some of us had expected originally, but we had
actually made it across the country, regardless of the shape we
were in. Sometimes it seemed like this mythical joke: "Where's
the Nomadic Festival?" people kept on asking. "Oh, we're
around. Just a little tired from being so festive all the
time..." Actually, we all scattered that week, running into
each other at events here and there. There was so much going
on in different places. There were always people in and out of
the Clark St. house which was the nerve center of the
gathering. A bunch of people went off to go get in trouble in
San Francisco and stay in this squatted building. Stephanie
showed up with Maria from New York and she and Arrow went off
to spend time alone together. Trevor decided to run off with
some hippies to a gathering on Mt. Shasta and that was the last
we saw of him. Sara and Harry decided to finally settle down.
There were so many new people around it felt like our ranks had
swelled about ten times.

THREE FREAKS, A
DOG, AND A PINK
FLAMINGO ——→

I think in everybody's eyes the gathering was a big success. The workshops were wonderful, there was plenty of food, it gave a lot of good people the chance to meet and play together, work on various projects. The time the organizers put into setting it all up really paid off in the end (although every time I ran into one of them it seemed like they were on the verge of insanity.) I think a lot of people walked away from the whole thing inspired to action.

The parade that Saturday was the culmination of all the time everyone had put into going to the workshops and building puppets and making flags and banners and masks and learning to walk on stilts and learning demonstration defence tactics. It was a massive "Parade Against Consumerism" down Telegraph Avenue and all over Berkeley, a spontanious celebration of life that wound its way around around the city and stopped a lot of traffic.

← THE PARADE AGAINST CONSUMERISM →

BORN OF FIRE

A GATHERING OF
HERETICS & LUNATICS,
AUTONOMISTS & TRIBALISTS
JULY 18-22, 1995
SAN FRANCISCO BAY AREA

WELCOME

To the Born of Fire conference/festival.

Our intent for this gathering has been to make manifest some of our ideals of self-reliance, anti-capitalism /consumerism, comunity, creativity, activism, & love.

Most of the workshops will be activity oriented, involving the teaching or enhancing of a skill, artistic exploration, or play. Our focus is empowerment; our goal, stronger selves, & better world.

The first three days of workshops will take place at 924 Gilman St, Berkeley. The fourt day will be outdoors in Golden Gate Park, San Francisco. The fifth day is tentatively scheduled as a picnic/celebration.

We chose the name "Born of Fire" for this event because our generation inherits & is the product of a threatened planet -- one which smolders under a depleated ozone layer & burns with the exhaust of a billion cars. Like the mythical phoenix, we can raise ourselves from this infer-

-1-

no, and, working together, perhaps restore hope for future generations. Learning to rely on ourselves and each other, rather than the offerings of mainstream consumer culture, is one step towards transcending the current order & healing our threatened earth.

This event would not have been possible without the wonderful help of many incredible people! If you helped out in any way, Many, many thanks.

ABOUT 924 GILMAN ST.

924 Gilman St. is a non profit, all volunteer punk venue that has been in existence since 1989. They have been very kind in allowing us to use their space on short notice when our original location fell through. After eight years they've struck an uneasy truce with the neighboorhood & the authorities. We are expecting you not to screw this up! If you cannot abide by their rules-- no drugs or alcohol in or around the club, no blocking the streets around the space, and no intentionally pissing off the neighbors (i.e. graffiti!!!) we will ask you to leave.

-2-

HELPING OUT
DURING THE EVENT...

WE NEED VOLUNTEERS TO:

- Cook Food Not Bombs in the morning and/or drive food to workshop location

- Volunteer for end-of day cleanup

- Go on dumpster-diving expeditions

- Provide accomodations for out-of-towners

- do security

- Carpool to workshops outside of the space, to Golden Gate Park (Friday) & to the Berkeley landfill (Saturday)

YOU CAN SIGN UP AT THE INFO TABLE! THANK YOU!

Also, please be aware that several people had to spend their own money for workshop supplies. We are counting on your donations to make crucial reimbursements! If you don't have money, at least sign up to volunteer! This event can't be a success unless everybody helps!

-3-

68

TUESDAY, JULY 18			
2:00–4:00	PIRATE RADIO	STAYING OUT OF THE DOCTOR'S OFFICE	COLLAGE	BICYCLE MAINTENANCE
– BREAK –				
5:00–8:00	HERBWALK	SHADOW PUPPETS	SPIRAL (3:00 GARDENS 6:00)	JEWELRY MAKING

WEDNESDAY, JULY 19			
2:00–4:00	SILKSCREEN	BANNER-MAKING	CLINIC DEFENSE	ACUPRESSURE
– BREAK –				
5:00–8:00	BEAT THE HEAT	INTRO TO HERBAL MEDICINE	PLASTER BODY CASTS	STENCIL-MAKING

THURSDAY, JULY 20			
2:00–4:00	? HEALTH	D.I.Y. FILMMAKING	A.K. PRESS	EVICTION DEFENSE NETWORK
– BREAK –				
5:00–8:00	SURVIVING RADICAL PRISON	BOOKBINDING	TOTEM MASKS	FIELD TRIP TO THE CLIFFS

FRIDAY, JULY 21			
1:00–3:00	TRIBAL PERCUSSION	WRITING WORKSHOP	SELF DEFENSE	FOOD NOT BOMBS
– BREAK –				
4:00–7:00	WOODWORKING	WILDERNESS/URBAN SURVIVAL	STILT WALKING	(STILL AVAILABLE!)

-4-

Workshops

Please check at the info table for workshop locations.

TUESDAY, JULY 18TH

HOW TO STAY OUT OF THE DOCTOR'S OFFICE - Educating selves about ways to take control of your own body & health.
2-4 PM

PIRATE RADIO - Free Radio Berkeley founder Steve Dunnifer will speak on the possibilities & realities of pirate radio. He will be discussing the local, national, & international free communications scene. A primer on how to start your own pirate station.
2-4 PM

COLLAGE MAKING - Piles of magazines, some glue sticks, & X-acto knives await you. Please bring extra supplies (if you have them) & your imagination! (Adam)
2-4 PM

BICYCLE MAINTENENCE - Maintenence & upkeep for two wheeled road warriors. (TBA)
2-4 PM

-5-

HERBWALK - A walk in the Berkeley Hills to become familiar with local plants & their properties. This will be preceded by a presentation about making these plants into medicine & herbal medicine in general. This is a practical, not theoretical workshop! Please sign up at the info table if you can drive people to Tilden Park. (Francine) 5-8 PM

JEWELRY-MAKING - Demystifying the art of crafting body jewelry. Multiple approaches provided by local & wandering jewelry makers. (Ian, Jeff, & John)
5-8 PM

SHADOW PUPPETS. Intro with demonstration/performance by Wise Fool Puppet intervention from S.F. Making shadow puppets out of cardboard & found materials - simple or intricate - to perform with later in week behind screen lit with torches. Bring X-acto knives & found stuff for hours of fun. (Aron, Anaconda Puppet Studios, Mpls.)
5-8 PM

SPIRAL GARDENS. Organic gardening on squatted land! Join Dan & other members of the Spiral Gardens Collective at the community garden on 59th bet. Market & Adeline (carpool may be available; see info. table for map & directions).
3-6 PM

-6-

WEDNESDAY, JULY 19

CLINIC DEFENSE - How to escort clients into the clinic, bypass blockades, strategies for dealing with Operation Rescue fascists, setting up clinic defense in your town, spotting fake clinics, & more! (Mimi)
2-4 PM

SILKSCREENING - Learn the basics of silkscreening and bring T-shirts, etc. for a screening party! (Karyn)
2-4 PM

FLAGS & STANDARDS - Tools & supplies provided for making standards, flags & banners to decorate our gathering space and make a statement during Saturday's parade! (Workshop conducted by members of the Black Maggot Crime Collective)
2-4 PM

ACUPRESSURE - Basic introduction to acupressure pressure points, body's energy, relieving stress & increasing energy.
2-4 PM

STENCILMAKING - Tools & materials provided. Customize the world with your unique vision! (Sean)
5-8 PM

-7-

PLASTER BODY CASTS · A creative, fun approach to molds & masks; we may have live background music, too! Bring paints, ornaments, plaster, vaseline, or things to cast, if you have them. (Stephanie)

5-8PM

INTRO TO HERBAL MEDICINE MAKING ·
How to make & use your own tinctures, salves, teas, & liniments. Processes will be demonstrated as well as described.

5-8 PM

BEAT THE HEAT · An interactive workshop, consisting largely of roleplays, covering arrests, searches & search warrants, police interrogation, how to manage your lawyer, and the difference in legal strategy between civil disobedience arrests & accidental arrests. (Workshop conducted by an anarcho-feminist, ex-con Harvard lawyer.)

5-8 PM

⚖ THURSDAY JULY 20 ⚖

BOOK PUBLISHING · Taking self-publishing a step beyond zines. A presentation by & question/answer session with anarcho-publisher Ramsey of AK Press.

2-4 PM

-8-

EVICTION DEFENSE NETWORK · We are a group that uses both legal & direct action tactics to combat homelessness & defend tenants, through fighting evictions. Find out why we've been successful & how to organize in your town to battle scumbag landlords, and win. (James Tracy plus other members of Eviction Defense Network.)

2-4 PM

WIMMIN'S HEALTH · Specifics of this workshop T.B.A....we may have a menstrual extraction video, & info covering herbs, infections, pregnancy, staying out of the gynecologist's, etc. (Heidi or Kristen)

2-4 PM

D.I.Y. FILMMAKING · Fundamentals of moving-image media. (Keith Evans) 2-4 PM

TOTEM MASKMAKING · Creating a mask of your own totem animal. Supplies will be provided but we could always use more fabric & sewing-type supplies. This would be a rad follow up to Wednesday's Plaster Casting. (Patience)

5-8 PM

📖 BOOKBINDING · Bookmaking for beginners. Along with a hands-on approach to Japanese & other binding methods, you will be shown how to put a standard book together from start to finish. (Matty)

5-8PM

-9-

SURVIVING RADICAL DEMOS · How to get through out-of-control demonstrations in one piece. (Mike)

5-8 PM

PACIFIC OCEAN FIELD TRIP · A beautiful, semi-secluded spot on the far side of San Francisco. Cliffs, trees, sea, & abandoned bunkers. See info table to sign up if you need or can provide transportation.

5-8PM

⚖ FRIDAY, JULY 21 ⚖

In Golden Gate Park! Not at Gilman! (see page 12)

FOOD NOT BOMBS · F.N.B. co-founder Keith McHenry will talk about how to start a Food Not Bombs, and give an update on FNB's current activities.

1-3 PM

TRIBAL PERCUSSION · Communicate energetically without words! Using percussion instruments & found items, we will explore the art of nonverbal conversation. Please bring percussion instrument or alternative. (Sam)

1-3 PM

SELF DEFENSE · A highly trained martial arts teacher provides some rudiments of self defense in & for alternative communities. (Mike)

3 hours: 1-4 PM

-10-

A GATHERING OF SCRIBES · Decentralize writing & publishing process! The content of this participatory workshop will be up to the attendees. Let's sit and write & write, share previous work, make a collaborative zine, etc. Open to those who don't identify themselves as writers. Bring a pen & writing surface if you can; we'll provide paper. (James)

1-3 PM

STILTWALKING · Stilts can turn any demo or protest into a spontaneous act of street theater or poetic terrorism. Learn how to walk with & use them. Please sign up at the info table if you plan to attend this workshop before Thursday if possible. (Andrea)

4-7 PM

WOODWORKING · An introduction to materials & tools, with a special emphasis on using found, recycled, & salvaged supplies. Special location for this workshop: 1661 Mission @ Plum (a couple blocks from 16th/Mission BART, or get directions at the info table). (Eric)

4-7 PM

WILDERNESS/URBAN SURVIVAL SKILLS ·
An open invitation to experts, semi-experts, & novices in these fields to gather & exchange tales & tips. Scams, squatting, dumpstering, edible plants, temporary shelters; you get the idea....

4-7 PM

MORE WORKSHOPS T.B.A?
Check info table for daily updates.

-11-

SPECIAL INFO ON THE DAY IN GOLDEN GATE PARK

On Friday, July 21, workshops are scheduled to happen at Marx Meadow in Golden Gate Park, San Francisco. By public transportation from the East Bay: take BART to the Powell st. station & take the #5 Fulton bus westward to 25th ave. By car, take the Bay Bridge, and follow signs on the S.F. side of bridge that say 'Golden Gate Bridge'. Get off at the Fell Street exit, follow Fell to Stanyan (bottom of G.G.Park), go right to Fulton, turn left, and take Fulton to 25th Ave. Workshops start at 1:00, but we'll be there at noon if you want to be early.

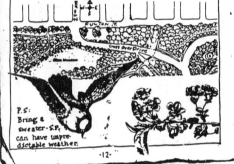

P.S: Bring a sweater-S.F. can have unpredictable weather.

-12-

TUESDAY, JULY 18:
- Concert at the Trocadero: Neurosis, Grotus, Logical Nonsense, Man Is The Bastard. 520 San Francisco (415)995-4600 ($10)

- Tropical Moonlight Gypsy Party Soiree: 7:30-8:50 location ??? call for info (510)420-1304

- Video at Chateau House: Death of a Nation. A horrifying documentary on the brutal genocidal Indonesian regime. Gives a historical look at Indonesia's attempt to eradicate the Timorese people, and their military support from governments like our own. (Presented by the East Timore Action Network) 9:00 PM, 2445 Hillegass bet. Parker/Dwight (1 block from People's Park). Free.

WEDNESDAY, JULY 19:
- Video at Chateau House: The End of the Nightstick. A video confronting police torture in Chicago. An intense, powerful, and inspiring documentary. Do not miss. (Video provided by copwatch) 9:00 PM, 2445 Hillegass bet. Parker/Dwight (1 block from People's Park, Berkeley). Free.

- Open Mic Performance Party: Bring yourself and your music, words, dance, or whatever. Bring some

-13-

chow to grill, hang out, have fun. Call Terry for Info: (415) 648-8740. (Free)

THURSDAY JULY 20:
Nothing yet to our knowlege! Sorry! Check at the info table for updates... Also, let us know if you have an event planned...

FRIDAY, JULY 21:
- Folly of Polly: The creation of a new diety. Bring food, costumes, offerings, etc. for a night of polyrythmic, polymorphic, polysexual play. The 848 Community Space: 848 Divisadero at MacAllister 7:00PM-whenever. (Free.)

- Concert at Gilman: Fifteen, Frail, Spirit Assembly, Matewan, Bisy Backsin. At 924 Gilman, Berkeley To work, 7:00 PM. Otherwise, 8:00 PM. $5, $2 membership.

- Mideast Vocal Instrument Dance Jam Party: festive hangout/class... an unconventional intro to gypsy belly dancing, mideast rythm, & more? Youth welcome. 729 Heinz #4, Berkeley. Info: (510)420-1304 7:30 PM? ($3-4 donation)

SATURDAY, JULY 22:
- Concert at Gilman: Avail, Rice, Siren, Gus, Tired From Now On. At 924 Gilman, Berkeley. To work (free admission)7:00 PM. Otherwise, 8:00 PM. $5, $2 membership

.. MORE EVENTS T.B.A?

-14-

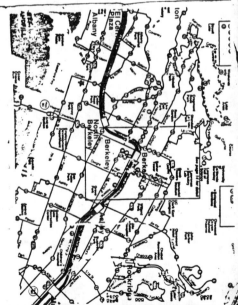

A couple of the nights during the gathering, me and Megan stayed in the attic of this house where these old friends of mine lived: Joe, Ellen, Rhea, and T-Fred. Their place was right smack on Telegraph Ave in Oakland and they had this huge horrible cigarette billboard right outside their window that they had to look at every day. All summer I'd been wanting to fuck with more billboards, twist pop culture slogans around so

the advertisments ate themselves. I still have this plan/daydream of traveling the country someday with one or two other people in a pick-up truck full of supplies and reworking signs all over the major highways. Anyway, one morning I finally went up and did an alteration on the thing so that it looked like the Angel of Death was carrying off this screaming, bloody woman.

The setting is Telegraph Avenue, it was 2:00am, the street was deserted, and I was just putting the finishing touch of black paint on when Ellen signaled for me to duck down. All of a sudden this police helicopter appeared out of nowhere and started shining its spotlight within a couple feet of me, circling around the roof like it was looking for its prey. It was totally loud and bright and scary. I looked around the Oakland city-scape and I felt like I was on the set of Blade Runner or one of those evil post-apocalyptic urban nighmare movies. As quickly as the copter had been there it was gone and I was left sprawled on the scaffold, my heart beating a mile a minute, totally confused but adrenaline happy they hadn't spotted me. We figured out later that some passing car must have seen me climbing up onto the roof and thinking I was breaking into the scuba shop next door, called the cops. They're hooked up, those 5-0 guys. I wish that every time some kid was getting beaten down on the street by police, we could have some crazy tech squatter helicopter swoop down and fuck them all up.

The Ride to Eugene

After the gathering ended and we all made plans to meet up in
Eugene in a couple days, me and Meg hitchiked to Roseville,
California. See, I had never hopped a train before and Megan
was gonna show me the ropes. Roseville's supposedly one of the
easist yards to hop out of and considering my bad luck (I sat
in a trainyard once in Belen, New Mexico for a day and a half
trying to catch a hotshot to Barstow before I gave up and have
be kicked out of numerous yards all across the country) we
decided to break the spell there.

Ever since I was 14 I've been wanting to hop trains. There were
always travelers passing through New York who would tell me
these crazy stories about riding the rails and I'd sit and
daydream through my little boring life about the day I'd
finally be riding on a train through the mountains somewhere in
the far off future.

So we got to the yard after four really good rides, one after
another, and found a good spot in the bushes right by this
bridge where the tracks head up to Eugene, and waited. We must
have been there for only two hours when we heard a bunch of
people walking towards us. It turned out to be the nomad posse:
Stacey, Pete, Dennis, and Dave. They had just hopped out of
Oakland a couple hours before and were all excited. So the six
of us waited together.

Memories of waiting in trainyards always seem surreal to me
because I never seem to sleep and it's always such a mystery
watching the trains move back and forth, wondering what they're
putting together and where it's going. Finally after the sun
had risen a train went by but we didn't get on cause we were
kind of in daze. We waited some more. I was talking to this old
hobo guy who was on his way to Portland when another train
started pulling out. He pointed out the only ridable car on the
train - a ribbed 48 - but said he wasn't in any hurry, so we
all made a mad dash and hopped in the bucket just as the train
started speeding up.

So six of us were all hanging out in this one 48 bucket. We
were all pretty much new at trainhopping, Pete and Megan a
little more experienced than the rest of us. This was some
badass shit we were pulling off. What's amazing about being on
the train is that you go through these places no one else ever
sees because there's no highway. Most of the lines are really
old, nineteenth century, from when the railroads were the only
means of interstate transportation. There's this feeling of it
all being really old - the hypnotic sound waves of the train
moving through the forest, metallic creaking along around
turns.
The first time we stopped, we were in the middle of these plum
orchards. We all got off and picked a bunch of these small,
yellow plums off the trees before the train started moving
again. We went across hundered year old bridges, riding above crystal
blue lakes and rivers. We watched the mountains appear out of
the distance till we were riding right through them.
It was my childhood fantasy finally come to life. I'll never
forget going through the Cascade mountains, sitting out on the
deck with everyone, watching a storm pass by us, lightning
cracking far in the distance, we were all smiling. That night
it was pretty cold but we all huddled together (we didn't have
much choice anyway) and watched the stars. When we woke up the
next morning, the train was just pulling into Eugene, Oregon.

It's like some crazy spy game - dodging the bulls,
hiding out in ditches, trying to figure out which
train to get on, learning about how the yards
work, hoping you know where you're going and
planning for where you might end up. It's a puzzle
- getting from point A to point B without getting
caught or lost. One of my favorite parts is
sitting there in the train car with the railroad
maps and the road atlas all blowing in the wind,
looking for clues as to where you are - piecing it
all together with glimpses of a highway sign or a
street name or a license plate or some major
landmark. The railroad maps have been out of print
for years but there are lots of bootlegged copies
floating around, grainy and confusing, detailing
intricate web-like veins of track around all the
major cities and big yards. A maze of confusion at
first, but there's this whole thriving underground
of people who ride the trains all over the country
and can tell you all the good spots to hide and
which yards are hot and what bulls to watch out
for how you know where a train is going and which
workers you can talk to and eventually you realize
you can get anywhere on the trains if you really
set your mind to it and you're really lucky.

FROM EVERYWHERE COMES

THE NOMADIC FESTIVAL's

THURSDAY JULY 27th 9 PM ALL AGES

CARNIVAL of CHAOS

MUSIC, THEATRE AND STRANGE IDEAS

WITH LOCAL GUEST FREAKS
THE AMAZING LANDFILL GARDENERS OF GONDWANALAND

ICKY'S TEA HOUSE   304 Blair

Eugene

Root Mugwart, a Eugene local who had been around in New York for some of the original planning meetings at Blackout, had set up a show for the Nomadic Festival that Thursday at Icky's Tea House. Icky's was the center of the radical universe in Eugene, a really good place to gather and meet people. A small shop with a good zine library and lots of folks passing through, a DIY bike repair shop next door, a porch to hang out on, a wide selection of herbal teas, a stage for shows, and really strong coffee, the folks at Ickies immediately made us feel welcome.

Our train gang was the first group to arrive but slowly over two days, the crews all started showing up. The momentum from the Born of Fire gathering managed to get a lot of people on the road and whole new group of nomads with new energy joined our posse. Weaving back and forth in the same places, we finally managed to hook up with the Atlanta crew. Black Box had done some crazy caravan trek along highway 1 with a couple vehicles. Red Thunder showed up with Stephanie - Arrow's partner in crime, Aron from Minneapolis and Mike from Tolstoy Village. Jill from North Carolina and her posse showed up. I don't remember exactly how, but Andrew, Steve, and his dog (God) Ghia showed up. Maria showed up with a carload of people. Everyone who was scattered all over in the Bay Area finally had a chance to be together in one place.

Instead of doing some separate show reviews, I thought I'd just write a little about some stuff that's been going on in Eugene that's on the weirder and noisier and ritualistic side of things since Ryder's got our punk/garage/indie scene really well covered. There was a big all-day festival planned in late July where Inter Sodalis and The Bella Low and Ekm Nola, among others, were gonna play on this side stage area. But it didn't have the right permits so the police came in with a chip on their shoulders and pissed off a lot of people. When they went ahead and arrested a guy who didn't want to take his booth down or give 'em us name, people started giving the cops a lot of shit. One thing led to another and the cops ended up blasting the crowd (at least 200, not all involved) with pepper spray. I personally know children who got sprayed. The crowd responded with a barrage of rocks etc. that injured 7 cops and sent 'em running. Draw your own conclusions. Anyway, there was no more amplified music that day...for a full written report on the incident write P.R.S., 440 Blair Eugene OR 97402. Later that week the Nomadic Festival rolled into town. This group of weirdos went around the country this summer as kind of an anarchist travelling circus roadtrip party/action. They put on a brilliant, life-affirming show at Icky's Tea House late one night with manifesto readings, rituals, elaborately costumed skits, audience/local music participation (The Landfill Gardeners, in a welcome return), acoustic punk songs about scabies, torches, shadow puppet shows, acrobatics, fire-eating, breaking glass, and dance. It was a really special appearance. The next night Tchkung! played at the WOW Hall and some of these things were reenacted by various nomads, who were added to the show at the last minute thanks to Inter Sodalis, the openers. IS sounded really low-energy to me that night, and the nomads didn't do the stuff I thought was best, but Tchkung! really brought the house down with an onslaught of drums, howling, and ambulance sirens. The people blowing huge clouds of flame in the middle of the dancing crowd were the finishing touch. In Au-

So first off I have to say that the Anarchist/Radical scene in Eugene is one of the most impressive and inspiring I've ever had the good fortune to encounter. I reckon it has something to do with all the clearcutting of the forests in Oregon, not to mention the whole Pacific Northwest, which is so massive and so obviously leading to eventual disaster that it's mobilized a large Earth First! movement that centers around direct action and is taken very seriously. It struck me that everyone around us seemed a lot more conscious of their connection and responsibility to the Earth.

Being a city-boy by nature (I didn't climb my first tree till I was sixteen years old and I grew up on the twelfth floor of an apartment building in the middle of Manhattan island), so used to concrete and smog and boxes of people stacked up on top of each other, it's a big deal to me when I meet people who know how to grow their own food and who follow the cycles of the moon and can list off all the indigenous plant species in their area. It's also hard for me to comprehend, not really being from a place where there are any trees, the speed at which the logging companies are cutting down the forests everywhere and the effect it's eventually going to have on all of us. But I can tell you that it's not hard to get angry when you ride the trainlines in Oregon past all the paper mills and patches of destroyed forest and then realize if everything continues at this pace, the trees are all eventually going to be replaced by strip malls and highways and track suburbs.

Another thing that I noticed about Eugene was that it has a pretty affluent liberal community ("new age" rags floating all over the place with advertisements of Yogi masters offering $400 workshops in enhancing spiritual and financial success.) Interesting enough, the social/economic climate had managed to feed the growth of a massive Food Not Bombs, able to maintain a five day a week feeding and house for a number of people on food donations, health food store dumpster scores, and door to door canvassing alone.

Also, I assume because the pace is so slow and the welfare is high and there is a pretty nurturing and welcoming radical community, there are a lot of cool people raising families. There are a bunch of little kids running around, something I'm not used to at all, which made me realize how important it is to have people of all ages around if we ever want to build a truly stable, working alternative community for the future. So many times radical scenes are made up of 15 to 35 year old, all transient and unstable trying to build for the future but always struggling with the present.

76

Not that there isn't struggle going on in Eugene. We all showed up at a really strange time. Not a week before, the Food Not Bombs collective had dissolved into two factions. Apparently, their substantial income brought ideological fights over how the money was to be spent. Money in a organization, no matter how radical, always seems to bring out really ugly shit. For once I was happy we were broke. One small group of people managed to take control of all the funds, got some land 45 minutes outside of Eugene, bought a minivan, and continued serving from there; setting themselves up pretty nicely in the process away from the original house that had been home to a dozen people and many a passing traveler. The rest of the FNB's people were very welcoming to us but were still feeling pretty angry over the split. At the last minute, a few decided to leave town with us.
On top of all the inner struggles, the previous weekend there had been a artists festival in a park without a permit that had turned into a police riot. Children had been maced and others had been beaten and arrested and the community was in an uproar. The tension was still really high in the neighborhood with the cops and Icky's, known as a trouble spot to the law, was trying to stay pretty low-key.

Most of us ended up camping out on the floor of the soon to be gone Food Not Bombs house. A bunch of people stayed at the Hillcrest House. In my eyes, it was really a great week, much more of what I envisioned the Festival to be like when we were first working on it. Lots of people coming and going, more political activity and inspiration then we had seen all summer, we had time to relax out in the woods and the hot springs, and we finally pulled off a great show.

ARON'S SHADOW PUPPET SHOW - ALTHOUGH I HAVE THIS SINKING FEELING THAT THE REPRODUCTION ISN'T GOING TO DO IT ANY JUSTICE...

Patchwork Shows

There was something really cool about our shows always being slapped together like some fucked up patchwork nomadic quilt. Always last minute. Always different depending on who was traveling with us. We were all talented in our different ways - some more visual and loud than others.

I couldn't breath fire or juggle, so I got up and used my writing and yelling as my performance. Everyone we traveled with did something. I like how Kathy's acrobatics got incorporated into the fire act. Or how Stergin got up all drunk and sang a song he wrote about being infested with scabies. Or how Tanya's wild dancing and Sean's kickass drumming just kind of fell into place once they started hanging with us. Or how Aron started traveling with us and his shadow puppet theater became the main part of our show.

The performance at Icky's had this amazing energy where it felt like the whole place was moving in rhythm together. People from the Hillcrest House had set up these gongs and these little kids were banging on them. Root was dancing around and blowing these huge bubbles all over the place. Stacey and Arrow and Tanya and Sean were all breathing fire. We did Martine's Goonybird skit, Pete as Dr. Zeuss with the 12 foot long pencil trying to erase Martine the Goonybird and Stacey the Lizard Boy. No one was sitting down watching by the end, everyone was part of it. After Aron finished his shadow puppet show, everyone went outside and continued the fire dancing. Sweaty and happy, standing outside after it was all over, I thought back to that first show in Cincinnati and realized we had actually come a long way.

Total Motion Sickness

Fly had sent my household a newsletter that had got us turned on to the Nom Fest conspiracy. It sounded like a stupendous endeavor. I wondered what sort of consociousness collisions this diverse mob might bring to our Atemporal Anomalous Zone.

As the fate would have it, my long desired visit to New York coincided with some of the final planning sessions being held at Blackout Books. I felt like I should check out these self-proclaimed nomads so that when I returned home I could help my bleary-eyed burg brace itself for the impact. This is how I became one of the Eugene contacts.

Through the meetings and fund-raisers and kick-off extravaganzas I became infected with enthusiasm for the project and became fast friends with Arrow and Sascha. I determined that I would help with what I could.

To that end lent my giant bubble making tools and skills and organized a frontal assult looting raid on Materials for the Arts (they never knew what hit them.)

I soon realized that uncertainty would be part of the festival. It was an effort to get even a tenative date arrival date out of anyone. I left town two days before the Nomads did, not knowing exactly what to expect or when.

- Flash Foward to Late July -

Should I go to the beach? But the Nomfesters will be here tomorrow. But this maybe my only chance this summer... I went to the beach.

I heard it was a crazy scene with sixteen people in my house. Good thing I wasn't there. I had booked a show at Icky's Tea House where anything can happen and spent my last three dollars making flyers that I posted myself. (It's OK, I'm a wageslave.)

The Icky's show was enchanting though brief. The Amazing Landfill Gardneners turned out to be just me blowing bubbles so sue me. I really dug Sascha's opening poem and the trippy shadow puppet show. Everybody loves a fire dancer. The show went so well that arrangments were hastily made to add the Nomads to the ¡Tchkung!, Inter Sodalis show the next night at the WOW hall (See accompanying review by Steve Bouton from the world renowned North-West indie-rock ragazine Snipehunt.)

As the revellers straggled away, life returned to the usual unusuals and I thought about my role in the whole thing. Of course my level of involvment was my choice and I realized I was dealing with New Yorkers, but everybody's (gross, gross generalization) attitide seemed to be "kick down for the festival man." with a slight insinuation that my wage slave existance was pathetic compared to their freedom and fun. This angered me more because they were right but still this trip couldn't have happened without people like me.

Humble and grateful travelers are always more welcome then those with demands and expectations. The Nomads would of course be welcome again but would do well to heed these words.

Love and Chaos,

Root Mugwort,

We are old. We are ancient. Our beliefs and ideas now called Anarchist Revolutionary were once common knowledge, spiritual base. We are young and spirited but wise with our reconnection to our foremothers and fathers. We can survive living off the waste of technoindustrial death culture - but we strive to create. To create our own culture of collective understanding, of collective sharing. We have goals. We will break down the walls that patriarchy has created to keep us apart, isolated. We will heal ourselves - our minds free of restrictions, our bodies free of disease, our hearts free to love universally. We are one! One mass movement of spirits seeking true freedom - on different sidewalks, beneath different trees, behind bars - but we are all one. We strive to create beauty in a world of grinding, gnashing mechanical uncleanliness. We think in terms of generations to come, how our grandchildren will live. We seek to reconnect with the ancient knowledge of our people overseas - the magic, the medicine, the respect for all living things - as stewards of our Mother Earth. We seek to learn of great Goddess' Kali, Baba Yaga, Ariadne, Aphrodite, Gaia, and others - their mysteries, their magic. For we need to return to our Mothers, the peacekeepers and givers of life. Patriarchy has disconnected us - encouraging us to rise up rather than ground ourselves, preaching and acting out a warring, egobased, terror society - where womyn are made to hate their bodies and discredit their minds. Where men are made to believe they are nothing if they don't prove themselves to be egotistical, arrogant, and aggressive - dominators of womyn and nature. We encompass Earth, Water, Fire, Air, and Spirit.

WRITE TO:
AMY SCHIMPF
115 EAST HILLCREST
EUGENE, OREGON 97404

We are old. We are ancient. We are one and continue to grow.

WE ARE ONE! - BY AMY S.

After we left Eugene, we spent three days relaxing and camping by different hotsprings in Oregon as we made our way up to Portland. Shedding our dirty clothes and layers of urban mental armor, we all lay naked in hot pools of water and sat by camp fires telling stories and getting to know each other better. There were four vehicles now traveling together and a trainhopping posse we were meeting up with in a couple days.

This page is dedicated to the four flat tires Red Thunder got between Eugene and Portland.

Something I haven't mentioned throughout this whole story is that Stephanie and Arrow were planning to raise a child together. Not knowing any of this when he sent the Nomadic Festival idea around originally, Arrow had been faced with conflicting responsibilities and enormous life-changing anxiety stuff the whole summer. After doing a bunch of soul searching in the time between Oakland and Portland, the couple decided to head back to New York with the van after we hit Seattle so they could get their lives in order and prepare for the awesome task of raising a kid. Which in the end I know was for the best, but at the time it kind of threw a wrench in our plans of world takeover (which I guess was kind of fading by this point anyway.)
 So that brings me to a short discussion about the tweaked dynamics in our group. Even in the most militantly anti-authoritarian anarchist group, there's always going to be subtle hierarchies and leaders and followers and all that nasty shit. Whether it's due to our natural instincts or outside conditioning is up for discussion, but there are always going to be people who take more responsibility and have more say and people who stay quiet and leave the important decisions up to others.

Luckily we didn't have too many things to argue about so there weren't so many power struggles going on. There were always new people joining along to fuck up any kind of stable power dynamics before they solidified anyway and we were all pretty much doing our own things, responsible for our own skins, looking out for each other but pretty comfortable on our own. Group coordination from a bunch of people who were used to traveling alone ended up being pretty ridiculous.

Our vans were the essence of chaos. A bunch of people's packs, stray garbage picked up from around the country and left to rot in corners, puppets, a disco ball, fireworks lying all over the place, dog food, people food, three huge rolls of this metallic confetti-type stuff that we could never find any use for, a box of bike tools, juggling balls, flasks of flammable firebreathing liquids, a pink flamingo lawn ornament that wouldn't go away, a bunch of silkscreens, paint, piles of zines and books and beer cans, a twelve foot long pencil and a bunch of oil drums tied to the roof, people and dogs and strange objects hanging out the windows, music always blasting, piling out onto the street ..

But see, what I was getting at before I went on that little tangent was that Arrow was kind of our figurehead. He was our fearless leader who everyone made fun of and wouldn't listen to just to piss him off, but he was one of the main driving forces in keeping everything going. No one wanted him to leave half-way through the summer. Besides which, he was taking Red Thunder and a whole bunch of supplies we couldn't carry on our backs with him and there was some question as to what we were going to do in the rest of the places we were planning to visit. What were we doing, anyway? In our attempt to do so many things at once, it seemed we lost any kind of greater focus and ended up always out on the street trying to make money to get to the next place we were going to have to struggle in.

So to cut it short, it was right about this time that the Nomadic Festival turned into one van full of people, a dog, and supplies - and a bunch of kids hitching and hopping trains, not knowing exactly why - but in the end it didn't really matter because we were all doing it together.

82

The Nomads dropped me and Megan off about a ten minute walk from the Vancouver trainyard. It was still light outside and we had a couple hours before we figured it would be safe to get on a train. We went and scoped out the yard, looking for a good hiding spot and checking the bull situation. I'm always really high-strung and cautious in trainyards. I get off on it though - sneaking around all covert, trying to piece the puzzle together without getting spotted. Megan always seems much more relaxed and cool about the whole thing, figuring we'll get on a train eventually I guess. I never think we're going to get away with it until we're outside the yard on a moving train.
"I don't know, seems pretty sketchy to me." (My line.) "Let's call Scotty in Seattle and see what he has to say, I saw a phone at that convience store aways back." When Arrow was first sending around the zine back in April and the vision of the Summer trek was first coming together, he had foreseen the problem of trying to cram a bunch of people with no gas money from every town we stopped at into a few vehicles. He suggested in the newsletter that people be prepared to trainhop and hitchike from to place to place. Then he added: "We do have a highly experienced young hobo who will be doing the whole route by freight train and has offered to take others if necessary." That was Scotty.

Scotty was kind of pissed about that and got up in arms every time it was mentioned. Arrow has this funny way with words sometimes, he likes to embellish things and has this laugh-"heh-heh-heh-fuck it, man - we can print that.." Anyway, I called up Scotty at his folks place and it sounded like there was a party going on. The first crew had arrived that morning and were busy getting down while his folks were away. "Hey Scott, we're right outside the Vancouver trainyard, how do we hop out of here?" What followed was a long description about anything I'd ever want to know about the Vancouver trainyard and then some shit I probably didn't want to know. "Well, let's see...walk down to that first crossing facing West, turn left, walk about thirty feet along the tracks, there should be some bushes and a swicher hut directly across..." Then he told me the crazy shit."Yeah, the yard you're in is big FTRA (legendary badass train gang) stomping grounds, so watch your ass. If you don't have any luck up where you are, walk about six blocks down on the other side. There should be a camp and a bunch of people drinking around a fire. Ask for Scrapper, Dutchman, or Babygirl. Say you know me and they should be able to help you out. But be careful..."

SCOTTY IN EURIKA SPRINGS

So we pulled it off with ease without enlisting the help of any old hobos and found ourselves on a super-delux Cadallic grainer car, on a North bound train. Woke up in the morning riding along the water and figured we were almost there. It was obvious we were pulling into some big yard and me, remembering something someone had said when we were still in Portland, decided it was time to get off the train. "Are you sure?" Megan said. "Amy told me we should get off before we pull into the Seattle yard, otherwise we're fucked." I replied like I knew what I was talking about. "Well, OK." I hopped off and Megan threw me my pack which landed in this swamp of green sludge. We both looked in horror as my pack submerged into a puddle of nasty shit.

Megan hopped off a couple seconds later but the train was moving fast and she was out of sight. She walked back to find me on top of a hill by the tracks with my stuff spread all over the place drying, cursing the world, cursing her (which was dumb and I was being an asshole, it was obviously a mistake), cursing my life. At least we made it, we agreed. This Native American guy with a 40 ounce came walking down to greet us. "You folks just get off that train? Yeah? Well, welcome to Tacoma." Fuck.

It was early in the morning and I was desparing, foreseeing us standing out on the highway all dirty, waiting hours just to go a few miles. I felt really stupid, too. But then this train went by and we said a quick farewell and hopped into a 48 bucket and stayed really low. We finally made it, and within a few hours we were at Scotty's folks house, lounging around relating stories and laughing all carefree like we had just been on some luxury cruise going up the coast.

THE BORDER

The setting is Downtown Seattle, Sunday night. We've all met up in Pioneer Square to have one last fundraising party together before Arrow and Stephanie make their trek back to New York and the rest of us head up to Vancouver. There's a little flaw in the plan though: Black Box is the only van heading up North and there are nine of us stuck without a ride. But this is a minor detail and there's lots of money to be made off all the drunk Navy guys passing to and from the bars on the strip. The fire show is unleashed and the buckets are getting full. Enter Jason - very large, maybe slightly tipsy, disgruntled Gulf War veteran with a big pickup truck. "I hate what this government did to me and I think what you kids are doing is great. Shit, I have nothing better to do with my night, any of you need a ride?" Fuck yeah we need a ride.

So after sad goodbyes to the East Coast bound couple and promises to meet up in British Columbia with the Box crew, nine of us piled into Jason's pickup truck and got a ride to the Canadian border: Me, Megan, Andrew, Steve, Melinda, Dennis, Amy, Mike, and Supa. Jason laughed and said it was like the Army trucks going through the desert in Saudi Arabia.

It was about 5:30 in the morning when nine dirty, slightly suspicious looking, windblown people with packs on their backs walked into the Canadian Immigration office. This woman, or more like this nightmare of a woman, took our ID's and we sat in these chairs waiting to get called up one by one and questioned. Before we walked into the office, we had worked out this story that was almost all true: we were travelers from the states going to Vancouver for a couple of days to visit our friend Martha and see one of our favorite bands, D.O.A., play at the music club La Quena at 1111 Commercial Drive. We had a ride back into Washington in two days and planned to spend our 48 hours in Canada exploring the sights and wonders of Vancouver and being all around model citizens, pouring what little money we had into the Canadian economy. Something to that effect, it was early in the morning and we hadn't slept. It seemed pretty easy and we strutted into the office nonchalantly. But this woman had it out for us. She interrogated each of separately about our reasons for entering Canada, our means of income, our permanent addresses in the States, how much money we had, how we had gotten to the border, our criminal history, why we were traveling together, did the mutt sitting outside have his shots and on and on... She dredged up these deeply buried ugly memories for me of the guidance counselor in my elementary school, condescending and snide and horrible.

EXIBIT A: THIS IS SOME FUCKING BULLSHIT.

"Oh, so you say you're going to 111 Commercial Drive? I see. Well your friend over their says it's 1111 Commercial Drive. So which one is it? 111? 1111? Come on, which one is it? And who is this Martha woman anyway? I bet she doesn't even exist. I'm sorry but your story is just full of holes. Next." One after another she saw us, and one after another she denied us. Then she called us all up as a group and lectured us. "I'm sorry, but none of you have proved yourselves worthy of being allowed into Canada. You don't have enough money as a group and I don't find you trustworthy..."

Two by two, we were all escorted via car with large, bald, gun toting uniformed chauffeur to the edge of Blaine, Washington. We had this image of Blaine being an entire town full of people who had been rejected from Canada and we looked forward to our welcome into the gang.

The sun had just risen and we all made our way to the local Denny's to plan our next move. We decided to try again in a couple hours when there was a new shift of people and a couple of us went and slept under a bridge until it seemed like the right time. We cleaned ourselves up a little, got some food, ate a bunch of blackberries and headed back.

I don't even remember if it was the same woman behind the desk, I was still really tired. It might as well have been. We took our seats and went up one by one all over again. When it was my turn for questioning I tried explaining to her that we all traveled around the country together and that we had made plans ahead of time to meet up with people in Vancouver and have a party. It was kind of like a network of people with common interests, I said. We all work together and they've provided places for us to stay, I said. I said a bunch of stuff, but after a while the woman just looked at me and said:

"I just don't believe your story. It's incomprehensible to me that nine people would be showing up to meet people they don't even know and that they'll all be guaranteed places to stay. I find it hard to believe that you all traveled this far across the country and you have so little money. As for this 'Festival' you've been telling me about, it sounds like a total fabrication."

"Don't you understand the idea of community? People helping each other out when they're in need? Don't you have any friends?" I was delirious and angry and losing my cool facade. "I feel sorry for you sitting in that little box all day, not knowing what it really means to live! Taking out the sorrows of your miserable life on a bunch of good people who obviously don't mean any harm. If I were you..." She cut me off: "Sir, do you want to come into Canada or not?" I exploded in a flood of profanity. "No! I don't want to come into your fucking country you horrible bitch! I don't want to have anything to do with you! I hate yo..." Someone pulled me away. The guys in the back were pointing at me, shaking their heads. I sat down and put my face in my hands, manicly laughing and muttering to myself.

A couple minutes later we were at a crossroads. Somehow, Supa, Andrew, Melinda, and Mike had all remained level-headed enough to pass the examination. Not having much experience with borders, it seemed so surreal to me that our fate as a group was being determined by some imaginary line that some of us weren't worthy to cross. It was starting to rain. Melinda decided to stick with us rejects and the three others wished us all luck and headed for Vancouver. Now there were six.

Dejected and wet, we made our way back to Blaine. It all seemed pretty grim. The guys we had seen hitchhiking a couple hours before were still standing by the on ramp, soaked and pathetic looking. We sat outside this convenience store at a gas station for a long time until finally, Melinda being very slick, managed to convince this motel manager to let us sleep in a room for the night, it being the off season and all. Relieved, we trudged into our luxury suite and all took hot showers and watched bad TV.

The next morning we had a choice to make: try and cross the border again, head East towards Mike's farm outside Spokane where he said we could stay, or head straight to Minneapolis. There was a 35 cent bus to Bellingham that left twice a day and it seemed like we'd have a lot better luck there. But it wasn't right that we had already come so far, only to turn around and head back the opposite direction. We sat by the traintracks eating blackberries and talking. "We're anarchists here, what is this border shit? We don't even believe in them. There has to be a way."

I called up La Quena and talked to Ryan. It turned out, because of some old legal problems he was worried about, Ryan had ███ Black Box drop him off in Blaine and he had ridden Pete's bike over the border, all the way to Vancouver. He told us to go about three miles out of town to Harvey Street, make a left until it dead ended, walk over some bushes, and we'd be right there. Damn, we can pull that off.

After me and Dennis scoped the place out, getting lost on someones property first and walking right past the border patrol office, we all decided on a plan of action. I called La Quena back and told Pete and Martine to pick us up on the other side in an hour. We took a taxi down to Harvey Street in two trips (the only cab company in Blaine and they didn't have a car big enough for all of us.) We told the cabbie we were meeting a friend by the Dead End sign at the end of Harvey Street, but I think he was pretty hip as to what was going down. Me, Amy, Steve, and Ghia we're the first crew in the cab and as we made that left down Harvey, we were horrified to see a border patrol car blocking our way. "Turn Around! Quick!" we said. "No problem." the cab driver smiled and made a fast Y turn, ready for action. The cop immediately started following us and put on his sirens. We pulled over.

This is the end, I thought. We're trapped. They're gonna lock us away and we're gonna rot and no one will know what happened. Should have just left town but it's too late. Never should have listened to Ryan fuck fuck yammer yammer yammer....

"Would you mind telling me what brings you all to the end of Harvey street this fine afternoon?" the border cop asked, motioning us to get out of the car. "Uh, we're supposed to meet a friend. We're not from around here. I think we're lost." I half-assed smiled. It wasn't working. "You kids are trying to get over to Canada, aren't you?" Acknowledging defeat, we all looked at each other and agreed: "Yeah, pretty much that's what's going on." The cop shook his head. He checked our packs for drugs and weapons and looked at our ID. After a couple minutes he said: "Well, I'm not gonna stop you if you want to walk over the border. It's not my problem. I'm here to make sure no one comes in. They'll have to deal with you on the other side if you get caught." Then he just drove off.

Well, shit. That was easy. No one wants us in their country. The cab driver was laughing. "You want me to go get your friends now?" "Sure." We hid in the bushes and waited. When they showed up, we decided one person should go ahead and meet Pete and Martine, rather than a bunch of people with packs walking up a mile to the major road swarming with Canadian border patrol cars. I was elected cause I was the straight looking one, no dreaklocks or piercings or any of that stuff, so I put on Dennis's green poncho and took the plunge into foreign territory, trying my best to look inconspicuous and Canadian (whatever that means.)

The air felt really fresh and everything seemed really beautiful, but I think that was only because I had spent the last twenty-four hours of my life determined to get over to this mythical foreign territory I wasn't supposed to be walking on. It was all farm land and there wasn't a single cop car anywhere. I made it to the road and waited, pretending I was invisible. The Black Box couple showed up a few minutes later and we drove back to the border. All commando style, we pulled over, opened the back doors, everyone piled in, and we drove off. No problem. Quick as lightning. On our way to join the festivities at La Quena.

So anyway, after all the bullshit, that's how we finally got into Canada.

re about this later in Aron's piece but the
ncouver gathering didn't turn out to be much
a gathering but more of a week long
aster.
Quena itself has an amazing scene of old
ftists and punks and various forms of free
inkers floating around and I highly
commend anyone heading towards the Vancouver
ea to check it out. Unfortunately, without
planned anything on our part, it felt as
most of the time are crew was just being a
isance due to our numbers: the kitchen staff
ild only use so many volunteer dishwashers
return for free meals and in any kind of
sup sense, we didn't put too much back into
e community.

Arrow, I received a copy of your Nomadic
Festival of mine in Vancouver, from where I
write. I am very excited about your plans; I think
it will be a great success! I have shared the ideas
with many.

I work in a non-profit leftist community
coffee house in Van. called "La Quena". None of
us get paid, none of us want to! This cafe is a buzz
of political activity. It started in '82, when mass
Chileans and Nicaraguans were fleeing the fascist
regimes in latin america, and is now a center for
fighting capitalism at home.

So, ideas for the festival;

Come to Vancouver. There is a small but
expanding scene here. We folks at La Quena are
attempting to organize a greater Vancouver area
revolution. It is the most interesting and enjoyable
work I have ever done! I would like to see more
attention brought to rent strikes, squatting,
dumpster diving, postering, etc. I am very interested in more information. I am anxious to get
things happening, and networking with folks.
Unidos Viceremos! Martha, Vancouver, B.C.

THE NOMADIC
ANARCHIST FESTIVAL
AUG 6-12

LIVE BANDS

OPEN STAGE

WORKSHOPS & OTHER CHAOTIC HAPPENINGS

251-6626

FOR MORE INFORMATION
DROP BY LA QUENA (1111 COMMERCIAL DR.)
FOR A SCHEDULE OF EVENTS

The one night that worked out really well was our takeover par
this abandoned building in some really sketchy part of town. A
bunch of us walked around the city with shopping carts that da
trashpicked a ton of junk and then we met up later at the buil
and created this monolithic sculpture out of it all. A couple
played that night and we interspersed our various performance
in between it all and the energy was really good. The sculptur
so beautiful that none of us had the heart to destroy it and w
ended up leaving it for the unsuspecting landlords who probabl
thought it was some satanic shrine or something.

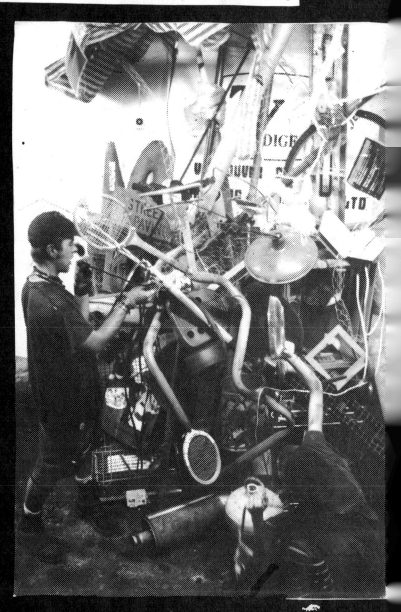

t all had this strange circularity
o it. It was early Sunday morning,

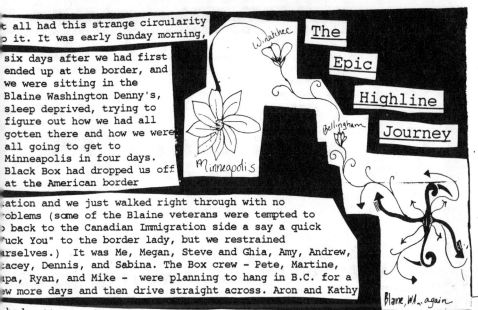

The
Epic
Highline
Journey

six days after we had first
ended up at the border, and
we were sitting in the
Blaine Washington Denny's,
sleep deprived, trying to
figure out how we had all
gotten there and how we were
all going to get to
Minneapolis in four days.
Black Box had dropped us off
at the American border

Winatchee

Bellingham

Minneapolis

Blaine, WA.. again

...ation and we just walked right through with no
...oblems (some of the Blaine veterans were tempted to
...o back to the Canadian Immigration side a say a quick
..uck You" to the border lady, but we restrained
..rselves.) It was Me, Megan, Steve and Ghia, Amy, Andrew,
..acey, Dennis, and Sabina. The Box crew - Pete, Martine,
..pa, Ryan, and Mike - were planning to hang in B.C. for a
..w more days and then drive straight across. Aron and Kathy

had gotten a ride to Bellingham from the Under the Volcano Festival and
were presumably on the road to the trainyard. We had plans to meet up
with them in Wenatchee, Washington, a crew-change point for the
Burlington Northern highline train - the mythical direct hotshot to
Minneapolis.

Five of us got on that 35 cent bus to Bellingham, leaving Amy and Steve
back in Blaine to search for Andrew who had crawled off to sleep
somewhere and then convince the next bus driver that Ghia was Steve's
seeing eye dog. We knew we were gonna have to split up to hitchhike
anyway, so it was alright.

When we showed up in Bellingham it was still really early in the
morning and none of us had ever been there. The folks who had picked up
Kathy and Aron had told us to go to the South Side of town, a place
called Tony's coffee shop, and that's where we'd have the best luck. It
was a few miles from the bus station, so we headed out along the road.
Me and Meg were lagging behind, stopping to eat the blackberries and
such, and Stacey, Dennis, and Sabina quickly disappeared from view. What
the hell, I figured, might as well get started, so I stuck my thumb out.
Not ten seconds later, a VW bug screeched to a halt in front of us and
we got in.

It was this aging hippie guy, looking like he'd been having a rough
time. Megan got in the front and I squeezed in the back, passing our
unsuspecting road friends very quickly. We told him we just needed a
ride to the other side of town and he nodded his head solemnly. After a
minute or so of silence, he said really cryptically "It's the end of an
era." Not so sure of his meaning, Megan asked him what he was talking
about. "Jerry, man, Jerry!" he sobbed. "He's dead." Not always the most
tactful person, especially early in the morning, I launched into a
tirade from the back seat about how Jerry Garcia had been a worthless,
fat old drug addict and it was probably better off now for him and his
followers that he had finally kicked the bucket. Megan told me later
when we were standing on the highway that the guy had tears in his eyes
and I felt really bad. Young people have no respect.

Anyway, he dropped us off and we found Tony's which was a sort of a
upper class cafe with a bunch of kids hanging out outside cause it
seemed there was nowhere else to go. The invincible trio showed up

and we all sat around for a little while and watched the rain outside that was just started to kick in pretty hard. Nice day for some quality hitchhiking. Yeah. We checked out the map for the hundredth time. Pretty straight-forward: South down interstate 5 to Everett - highway 2 East to Wenatchee. About 200 miles. Finally this guy overheard us talking and said he was heading down to Everett but he only had room for three people. Me and Megan acknowledged we had the unlucky number and it was time to head out to the interstate. We said goodbye to Dennis, Sabina, and Stacey and that was the last we saw of them till Minneapolis.

The highways in Washington have these big signs just past the on ramps with a crossed out thumb that say "NO HITCHHIKING" in big letters. We walked a little past the sign and watched the cars whizz by, contemplating sleep and willing ourselves invisible everytime a cop drove by. Finally, this guy who entertained us with stories of visiting prostitutes in New York and playing us the latest Seattle "grunge" music and kept on asking us if we had any pot even though we kept on telling him we didn't, gave us a ride to Everett. I could tell the whole time Megan was restraining herself from clawing the guy's eyes out.

He dropped us off and we walked across this old bridge to highway 2. This VW bus honked at us while we were walking and we could see it pull over aways ahead. Joyfully, we ran to catch up with it, expecting kind hippies to be waiting at the end, offering us drugs and food. When we ran up to the bus all out of breath, the door swung open and it was Kathy and Aron, beckoning us inside. They had gotten a late start on the day after spending the night relaxing in Bellingham. Everything that happened from that point on was total lunacy.

Their ride dropped us all off a little ways further at a farmers market by the side of the road. Immediately, the four of us caught a ride in this young farmers truck out of town and he showered us in fresh peaches and apples and left us at a really good spot. We waited for a few minutes and then this big black car skidded to a halt next to us and this really scary looking biker guy with tattoos of knives and skulls all over his arms leaned out the window and said: "Get in." We did. The really scary looking man, who totally lived up to his appearance, told us this story about how he had thirteen kids and his wife had just left him for a nineteen year old "nigger." It's pretty much the code of the road that when someone picks you up and they start spewing all sorts of fucked up trash you remain silent and nod your head. So we all listened to this miserable story of inbred hell in silence, driving really fast through these beautiful lush, green mountains. Every time Mr. Scary guy would pass a car that was going slower than he was (every single one of them) he would start yelling "Motherfucker! Get the fuck out of my way! I'll kill you! Fucking people just don't know how to drive around here..."

We had been driving for about twenty minutes when we saw Amy, Steve, Andrew, and Ghia by the side of the road. It happened so fast that all I remember is whizzing by, locking eyes with Amy for a split second, her eyes getting all wide, and then us all turning around to see them laughing and pointing at us. There was something really magical about that day. Even though we kept all splitting up along these roads we'd never been through, we were traveling the same path, destined to run into each other at the end of the line. It felt very much like some weird modern road fairy tale. Hitchhiking is like throwing yourself into the hands of fate, you never know who's gonna offer you a ride or where you're gonna end up. But if you're meant to get somewhere and you're determined, you'll get there by hook or by crook.

The scary racist guy dropped us off next to the only general store for miles and turned off on some dirt road. Everything around us was wet and green. Although the rain had stopped hours ago, the sky was still that eerie Pacific Northwest white - overcast and bright. It felt like the day had been going on forever but it was only about two o'clock. We filled up our water bottles and bought home made ice cream cones - chatting with the curious old ladies. Found a ride in the back of this guys pick-up truck with these two other local girls on their way back to Wenatchee who hardly said a word to us. As soon as the truck stopped the two girls ran for the road and got picked up by the first passing car. We were literally on top of a mountain and it felt like it might start snowing at any second. We decided to get with the program and me and Aron stood out of view while Kathy and Megan held their "two desperate beautiful women in need of rescue" thumbs to the wind. Like magic, a Winnebago like RV thing stopped and this old man came out and gestured us inside.

If the man was disappointed there were two more unexpected passengers, he didn't show it. I sat up front and talked to him while we drove through the mountains and everyone else dozed in the back. He was 75 years old and had worked for the forest service most of his life. When he had retired, he and his wife had bought the RV and traveled the states together. She had been dead for a number of years and he just kept moving, spending time at trailer parks and on friends' land, heading south in the Winter. I'd never been in a Recreational Vehicle before. There was a kitchen, a bathroom, a bed, a table, gas mileage was about as much as Black Box - the guy was hooked up. But he had no one to share it with and was obviously very lonely. We said goodbye and he dropped us off at Leavenworth where we all caught the free bus to Wenatchee.

Figuring we were way ahead of the game, imagine our surprise when we ran into Steve, Amy, and Andrew at the bus stop. They had passed us when we were back at the general store eating ice cream. We all hugged and related our travel tales over Taco Bell food, wondering about our other friends whereabouts. By now it was starting to get dark and we gathered more food and more water before we hit the train yard together. We found a good spot by the tracks at the edge of the yard and talked quietly, no sign of bulls. Aron was the only one of us who had ridden the line before and he entertained us with stories and Johnny Cash songs. We waited all night, sleeping restlessly to the sounds of the trains pulling in and out of the yard, seven people and a dog all huddled together.

Next thing I remember is our train leaving and trying to get my legs to run but having them not working quite right and stumbling all over the place. The rest of us were having the same problem but Andrew and Aron managed to hop into a 48, leaving five of us back in the yard as the hotshot took off. Disgusted at our splitting up the crew royal fuck up, miserable at the prospect of waiting in Wenatchee for another twelve hours, and scared about getting popped for trespassing now that it was daylight and we looked a little suspect all dirty with our waterbottles dangling from our packs, the five of us crawled under the porch of an abandoned restaurant further up next to the tracks.

the roads
the tracks
they go in circles
bringing us back
to tighten
old bonds

the roads
the tracks
they are part of our cycles
bringing us back
to start anew

the roads
the tracks
they never end
bringing us back
sisters, brothers, lovers, friends

BY AMY

93

We waited, dazed and quiet, lying down by this old mattress under the porch. Amy went off to go get a pack of tobacco or something and hoped the train wouldn't come while she was gone. It did. It was a split second decision. Andrew stayed back to wait for Amy while Me, Megan, and Kathy got on the train with a mix of relief and disappointment. As we pulled out of the yard I remember thinking how crazy it was that it was only 24 hours and we had split up and regrouped and split up so many times already. The three of us sat and watched the amazing forest of central Washington go by as we prepared ourselves to spend what we figured would be the next 70 hours together.

When we pulled into Spokane, we sided in a mess of tracks next to at least twelve other trains. It was a huge yard. We got off to explore a bit and found Amy and Steve and Ghia, hiding beside the wheels of a semi in a piggyback car a couple feet behind us. Amy had heard the train coming from town and ran back just in time for them to get on. Just as we thought this was the highlight of the century, Andrew and Aron appeared out of nowhere and suddenly we're all back together again just as the train starts moving.
So it was a beautiful ride and we'd earned it. Passing through the tip of Northern Idaho along a river, we all sat together in silence listening to the sound of the train moving along the old tracks. As the sun was going down we were pulling through Glacier National Park in Montana, the moon rising to our East illuminating the mountains and the water. The next morning we all got kicked off the train in Havre Montana and all got back on piggyback cars on the same train just as it was pulling out. That day we rode past fields and fields of sunflowers pointing up at the sky all through North Dakota. Before it got dark the second night, we all crawled on our stomachs through the cars to meet up with each other and eat dinner together. The train pulled into Minneapolis two nights later and we all got off and made our way to the Hard Times Cafe, covered in diesel grime and happy. That, my friends, was The Epic Highline Journey.

MINNEHOPELESS (as some folks fondly refer to it..)

So by the time we all converged in Minneapolis, the Nomadic Festival had kind of been reduced to a pack of tired kids hanging out at this late night coffee shop on Riverside and 19th. Any last little glimmering illusions of grandure that might have been left over had finally worn off on all sides by this point and the idea of trying to coordinate any further group trek towards Wisconsin just sparked groans and whimpers from the tattered crew.

Aron housed most of us at his
Anaconda Puppetry Arts Studio space
(what used to be the Emma Center
space before its demise) where
we camped out on the floor
for a couple

nights together and ate nasty
donuts from the convience
store dumpster down the street.

ARON'S SHADOW PUPPETS IN FULL FORCE →

THE ANACONDA PUPPETRY ARTS STUDIO SPACE↲

NOMADIC FEST TWIN CITIES

ART IS NOT A DIVERTISSEMENT, IT IS A PART - AN ESSENTIAL PART OF THE RESISTANCE.

ART IS FOR LIBERATION, FOR LIFE, OR IT IS FOR NOTHING.

The high point of the week by far was Steve the Fire Guy's (see his accompanying ramble) pyrotechnics workshop which combined the best elements of lecture and hands on practice (after a discusion of various chemical combinations and videos of things he had blown up in the past, Steve taught us all how to make cardboard cherry bombs and tin can smoke grenades.)

STEVE'S WAREHOUSE

PETE BUILDING A SMOKE GRENADE

AMMONIUM NITRATE SMOKE GRENADE

Chemical	Parts by Volume
Crushed Charcoal	3
Crushed Ammonium Nitrate	2
Sulfur flour	2

Combine the above ingredients and mix well. Punch 8 or more small holes in any size can and cover each with a drop or two of wax, except for one hole to thread the fuse through. Knot a safety fuse at one end and thread through the hole at the bottom of the can (save the top of the can for later) with the knoted end on the inside of the can, about on third of the way in from the direction of the hole. Secure the fuse with epoxy. Load the composition into the can, packing it tightly until the can is nearly filled. Reinsert the top of the can (it will now be the bottom) and secure with epoxy.

WHERE'S THE FIRE?

...It isn't around here, that much I'm sure of. Here in Minnesota, The Land of 10,000 Lakes and even more dry chemical fire extinguishers, the fear of fire is an institution well worth torching. If only the job were listed on the mainframe at the St. Paul Job Corp., I could finally be a team player... for the other team. Let fire rain down on the freshly paved streets of this city, to set aflame their asphalt surfaces, then spread upward to engulf that hideous homage to Star Wars and Habitrail, the skyway system. It's the most extensive in the nation, one postcard claims. The Twin Cities also has one of the coldest winters in the U.S., so where's the fire? No one gives a shit about the skyways, even when they're making constant use of them to avoid the deadly wind-chill on the street. Then again, you aren't supposed to care. The skyway and its invisable central heating unit are how the Twin (fraternal) Cities say, "Wouldn't you really rather have a Buick?" and "Mastercard, I'm bored."

Fire, it seems, is too dangerous a friend to be seen with in most cities, even though she's a good friend, it should be said. She keeps us warm at night and cooks our meals, but we neglect her. There was a time when we could look her in the eye, confess our love and get close enough to feel her breath. Not anymore. Our liaisons with her aren't keeping her happy, either. That burning man thing out in the desert just isn't cutting it, and the Fourth of July is a joke, pitched by the state to get us to look up

in the air.

CONTACT STEVE:

500 N. Robert St. #706   St. Paul, MN 55101 U.S.A.
Phone (612) 222-7911   Fax (612) 698-3922

98

Before we all went our separate ways and scattered across the country, fifteen of us all got tattooed together from these somewhat sketchy guys who offered to work on us for free cause they needed practice.

Fifteen of us are marked for life with a little symbol Stacie drew up to remind us of our crazy Summer traveling with the Carnival of Chaos.

ARON + SQUISH: MADMAN.

I'm not feeling quite so eloquent at the moment so I'm going to let Brother Aron take over the narration for a little while I go stick toothpicks in my eyes and lay out the epilogue.

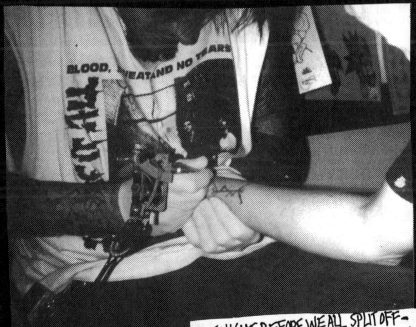

BLOOD, SWEAT AND NO TEARS

THE NIGHT BEFORE WE ALL SPLIT OFF — AT THE OMNI TATTOO PARLOR 26th & CHICAGO

JUST ONE PERSONS POINT OF PERSPECTIVE ABOUT ALL DAT. BY ARON
My ramble for the report on NO-MAD-DICK FEST-IV-FALL and my
participation was from Oakland to Mpls, the last half of this
first attempt at a travelling-self-sustained brain storm of
performance, exsistence and instinct. [Of course this is a
regular occurence in Europe, but give us a break, this is the
United States of An indecision.]

I was stoked to know that what was initiated had actually
got off the ground and was taking place to some degree. It was
part of the bug that bit me into hooking up into the on-the-
move many headed amorphous hyrdra of a road show. In this rant
I intend to be speak freely about my honest opinions--both
positive and negative, constructive and maybe even a bit
deconstructive if I happen upon a tangent.

It is always beautiful to see any much-discussed idea finall
given fuel and a vehicle to overpower the coming of any fear
-apprehended actions. Many of the people involved with this
thang at one time or another have crossed paths in similar
situations at some point in time, even with everyone being on
different levels and from various backgrounds; we still seemed
connected within the same multi-layered under(play)ground.

It could have been any given dozen or more freax figuring
out this thang along the way. That's exactly what we need more
of now, and pretty much how we all got by--just by doing it,
even without much money or practice. Anyway, in one strong sl;
of my view, it worked out well overall, in other ways, I thin
it failed itself in some aspects. This is only from my part
of participation and what I know from discussing the other ev
I wasn't at with people who were.

Okay, so I ended up in Oakland two weeks before the Nom Fest
stop at the Born of Fire Gathering. Puppetry has been my thing
as of late, so I offered what I knew and could do. It turned
out to be a fairly successful shadow puppet making workshop
at Gilman. About a dozen people made rad cardboard creatures
and along with what I could create, it turned it to a series
of shadow show/demonstration/performances in Berkeley which
led me to take what was made to other scheduled places on the
Nom Fest. In the Bay Area, the Born of Fire Gathering went really
well, not necessarily an @-fest, but more of a meeting of minds
to share knowledge on specific how-to-do projects. The result
seemed to be more poignant than the pointlessness I've felt
at Anarchist gatherings where things can get too intellectual
or lost in redundant rhetoric. Anyway; I put out my thanks to
all helped out without in anyway...

Upon arrival, the Nom Fest seemed to scatter out thru the Bay at not much of a solid presence at the B.O.F. thing, but I still joined in with these friends at a few fun street performances in Berkeley and S.F. There were some extra-special occurances amongst that shift, yet local people didn't seem too impressed. It was hard to tell who was a part of what, or anything at all, for that matter, especially from a more distant glance. What was contributed to any sort of community?, was question I heard asked, as it could appear more was taken by the larger nomad posse than given back in the end. And that kind of question could have been raised just about anywhere they(we)(I) went. Sure, the original core left from New York with no money and made down, up and around to Mpls with various means and ways, but what was left in the wake besides pulling off a good time? I guess it depends on the perspective, eh?

We probably all have different answers and reactions to thes questions, and mine changes at times. Maybe we alienated cool hosts who won't want to deal with helping out future Nom Fest possibilities? I don't know, I'd like more feedback on this.

From Berkeley, the No Minds headed for Eugene, and I went along with the puppets produced by all. The show at Icky's teahouse, was, well...can I say RAD?! The sequence of skits performed flowed like wildfire, everyone merged to make it happen in some way. It felt the most festival-like of stops. Or maybe it was just that ICKY's coffee cut with who-knows-what. Thanks goes out to Sunshine and Gondwana folx.

Personally I really got into making the puppets come alive in both skits for the apreciative crowd, especially with the focused help of 6-month pregnant Stephanie. In the first one I used words and hassled the audience by making them laugh at themselves slapstick-style. It's a Punch and Judy style take off with squatters vs. cops and the power play between evil businessmen against poor panhandlers. The other skit is more steeped in what I now call "Animysticarchy". No words halt the gates to the subconscious by presenting strong images in movement sequences to the heart of resonant sounds and percussion. I don't know if any photo's will make it into this issue, but hopefully the picture is sort of painted to those not present.

Some of us also performed at a Tchkung show there, which turned out alright, yet was hard to translate ourselves into the "show" setting which required strict attention to forced timing for something more organic in nature.

101

Okay, so to balnce out all this positive stuff, one thing that pissed me off was the all-too-occassional lack of respect as guests in hosts homes. I don't want to personally slag anyone, but sometimes the (drunk) group dynamics were fuckin' flakey and left sour impressions in some places we stayed. Oh well, people will get over it, right? But will those same people kick it down again to the next Nomadic Festival? And while I'm going off, I might as well mention that I thought the Nom Fest was often bogged down by people not carrying their weight and a little more for that matter. It was a freestyle thang, so of course people could do what ever the fuck they wanted, but sometimes the general order of many days was to do nothing but drink and recover from drinking, me myself included on a few of those occassions. I'm not trying to come off as self-righteous at all, yet I get annoyed when I feel guilted by association in this travel situation where many people latch on more for the party than the creative/productive action-oriented stuff. So if it matters, I apologize to anyone who tried to host us and felt dissed in any way by this presence I speak of here.

Of course, there were fruitful occurences and exchanges that happened all along the way to counter that shit out, some of which maybe I wasn't on the fest for just yet. But I'm still afraid that the negative stuff didn't get dealt with.

HARPY EAGLE

SNAKE

Well, the hot springs in Oregon gave us a chance to get naked and chill the fuck out for a spell before the last leg of the tour. It made me remember even more that the woods are much more worthy than the shittycityscene, except that I began to wonder if our presence was as equally a nuisance to that environment as well. Okay, enough bad vibes brother...

On up the NW coast, there was nothing exciting or worthy to speak of in Portland, seems like that town is on the downturn No opportunities arrived or were created for us to thrive, just surviving and getting by. It is where the big decision was made by Arrow to drop out with one of the vans after Seattle. It brought up a challenge but didn't stop the fest from flowing on.

Hurry up and wait yet we made it to Seattle which I dreaded because of its hardcore anti-panhandling/street people laws. But much to my suprise we took over Pioneer square and made $90 two nights in a row doing fire-drumming and performance panhandling--sucking money out of drunk navy boys for a our gas bills. I met my surrogate psyhic gramma there who did straight shots of coleman fuel followed later by dogfood. She wanted us to go on the Ed Machmahon show with her and asked for a ride to New York, yet we had to decline. The 2nd night Seattle caught up with us and we had to bail after a surreal night of blue dog biting Navy boy, Arrow and Martine punching him out, and then the escape from attempted capture of the infamous blue dog by the forces of evil. We got out without arrest and headed out that night for Vancouver.

Vancouver was a tale of lost expectations. The organizers from La Quena cafe thought that 60+ people were to arrive, yet only 17 of us were lucky enough to straggle in over a few days. There was some mixed mutual dissapointment between us and the cafe, but many moments fused actions-sometimes it felt good, yet other times a waste of time. But it all ended with a bang so I left with some new friendships and a sense of worth. I got to do another shadow show before Assuck played for some punx who have rarely seen puppetry. The next night culminated with crazy performances at a space we squatted for the night. It was an occurence that we never could have gotten away with very often in the states. Someone tipped us off about the place so we took it over night for a TAZ party that turned out fun.

Many of us made it Minneapolis for the weekend of events planned but it was sort of anti-climatic because the fire show was cancelled due to permit problems and such. I was too burnt by then anyway and needed to chill. Steve Rife did a very informative pyrotechnic workshop but that was about it... Everyone decided to split off at this point, melancholy to see each other go, yet we knew it was time to do whatever else we wanted to do. I felt a certain momentum left over from it all so I plugged in deeper to puppetry and attempted to recuperate in the same breath. All in all, despite my criticisms, I'd

do it all again, just with → some minor reservations and more developed situations, or even something completely different for that matter.

→ the travelling puppetry tour will be happenning for sure some time over the next few years -- sooner or later -- possibly next summer, so write me if you are interested about it or the ANACONDA PUPPETRY ARTS STUDIO SPACES PO BOX 7302 MPLS, MN 55407 c/o ARON

BOMB SIDE PANEL

Staring at my tattered road atlas - open to the Wisconsin page.
The cover's torn off. The page with New Mexico and New Jersey
is lost somewhere in the desert. All the edges are folded up
and dog-eared. The left half of the United States is separated
from the right and probably soon to be missing. Both Dakotas
and part of Eastern Montana have been eaten by the rain and
rubbed away.//So what's left of the Nomadic Festival after two
and a half months looks like it's breaking up here in
Minneapolis. We've been so many places in such a short period
of time that I'm always forgetting where we are, what city
we're in, what month it is, what we're supposed to be doing.
Here at the end, I gotta say, there's this total relief that I
don't <u>have</u> to be anywhere next week. It makes we wonder if we
tried to do something that shouldn't have been done. When I was
hanging out with Jessica in Seattle a couple weeks ago I was
telling her all about what we'd been doing all summer (I think
I was still in high school the last time we really talked) and
she said: "You <u>would</u> need to write yourself a schedule to
travel." Maybe she's right. We created this thing for ourselves
and spent all this time trying to carry it out and here we are
at the end all burnt out and I'm not sure what we have to show
for it except some good stories and the lessons of the mistakes
we made for other people to learn from. That drive to move at a
fast speed, to travel like we do from town to town - it comes
from a desire to throw ourselves into new situations all the
time - never stagnate or solidify into a mold - but in some
ways it took the fun out of traveling because we knew where we
were going to be every week and had no chance to deviate from
the path. Maybe if we had our shit togehter more and had
something real to give back to all the people we stayed with I
wouldn't feel like my brain was so fried but I wonder. I hope
someone out there was inspired by what we did.

Journal Entry: August 22nd 11:30pm Chicago

's been one of those really crazy fucking days.
started about 9:00pm last night in Minneapolis
en Me, Meg, Dennis, and Kathy said goodbye to
e Nomad crew at the old Emma Center space. This
ght be a really strange metaphor and the more I
ink about it, the more it has these weird
saster implications - but it felt like those
ctures they showed over and over again on the
vs when I was in elementary school of the space

NASA

shuttle Challenger explosion - little pieces flying off the side
of this huge fire in the sky. We were one of those little chunks.
//Aron dropped us off outside the trainyard in his grandpa's old
pick-up truck and we walked all cautious and quiet - ready to duck
under one of the three semi's right by the tracks and wait for our
glorious Chicago-bound hotshot chariot.-Totally out of the blue (or
more like the black, mosquito infested night) we ran into Brendan,
Unrulee, and this guy Drake, on their way to Dreamtime Village.
What the fuck? Spontanous Anarchist Gathering in the Minneapolis
trainyard! Maybe. We hung out for two hours getting the shit bitten
out of us by some nasty Minnisota breed of trainyard mosquitos and
relating travel stories and common connections. None of us had ever
hopped out of the yard, but we all heard East bound trains would be
heading out on the first four tracks, so we waited. It was so
ironic to meet Unrulee just as the NomFest was breaking up. The
entire summer we kept showing up in the same towns where his
schoolbus had just left. The one time we were in the same place as
the bus was in Atlanta, but he wasn't even on the bus. Originally
co-conspiritors, he and Arrow had had very different visions of the
festival and I think had had some sort of falling out or
miscommunication thing before we left New York so I didn't even
know to much about the guy except that we were on similar paths
with different groups of people.//The last time I had seen Brendan
was very briefly in San Francisco when everything was so hectic at
the Born of Fire gathering. The Red Thunder crew had stayed on his
land in Southern Oregon for a little while before we all met up in
Eugene, but that was the last I had heard of him.

Anyway, we finally saw a hotshot pull into the middle of the yard
and we all climbed over three or four stopped trains to get to it.
We split up into two 48's and then did a whole lot more climbing
around when we realized the train had no engines. Fuckin A. I
finally got up my nerve and asked a worker if they were building
any hotshots to Chicago and he told me we were on the right train,
they were just fueling up the engines. Then he looked straight at
me and sternly said: "But be careful. They're looking for people
like you." I thanked him and walked back to the train with a big
smile on my face (people like me, that's right, people like me -
better watch out for us, never know what we'll do...) Within half
an hour we were out of the yard.

I fell asleep and have a vague memory of the Dreamtime crew hopping out at La Crosse and Brendan smiling. Then it was morning and me and Meg woke up along the Mississipi - felt really good. Dennis and Kathy were still asleep so the two of us just watched the morning sun fleck off the water and villages of lilypads go by. We figured we be in Chicago by the afternoon. The train stoppped briefly in Davenport and then didn't stop till we were in the middle of some cornfields. Dennis woke up and said he had just dreampt we got busted and kicked off the train. We all laughed. I jumped off the train to piss, just as these two fat ugly bulls pulled up in an unmarked car and started yelling at us to get off the train. Shit. So we find out we're in Chadwick, Illinois and we're slummin. It's some tiny shit town in the middle of nowhere and we're the most exciting thing to show up all month. So the four of us are sitting there, trying to find Chadwick on the map and getting our ID's checked. The town police show up, the county police show up, the state police show up, and they're all standing around socializing with the train police and checking our bags. The train leaves. We're informed there are no buses, we can't get back on the train, and we can't hitchike, so we better start walking. We said our goodbyes to the mass of police who showed up to greet our arrival and walked to the road. Finally some kind soul picked us up and drove us to the highway and we had some crazy luck getting to Chicago.

We got a ride most of the way there with some radio announcer guy who lived out in the suburbs and picked us up in his minivan. Then we got a ride in a limo which is something you only here stories about (like this one.) Then, this Mexican gangster guy picked us up in his pick-up truck, showed us his tattoos, and said he'd take care of us. He drove us to his neighborhood in West Chicago and brought us to his friends Mexican restaurant and fed us really well. All the kids there were flashing these strange hand signals to each other and looking at us funny. The guy was really cool and obviously had a lot of money and respect among the people. He was showing us off as his new friends to everyone. After a tour of the neighborhood and sad farewells, he dropped us off at the train station and gave us money to take the commuter train into the city. It's a couple hours later.

THE LIMO RIDE

DENNIS ↑

Kathy and Dennis are probably sitting in the trainyard right now and hopefully on their way back to New York. Me and Megan are sitting here in deserted downtown Chicago, waiting for a bus to Wicker Park.

MEGAN + HALF OF KATHYS HEAD ↑

LIMO GUY ↑

KATHY'S TRAIN STORY

The journey home

After the Minneapolis to Chicago adventure Sascha described in his journal entry, Dennis and I were ready to head all the way East ASAP.

Keep in mind that everyone we encountered along the way: the Chadwick Police Department, the guy who rescued us from Chadwick, the pretty woman with the baby, the nice old man, the radio guy, the limo driver, even the Mexican banger who toured us through Gangland; everyone warned us to "just stay out of South Chicago." So where do we have to go to hop out? South Chicago.

We said our farewells to Sascha and Meggin, then caught a bus dropping us there around one in the morning. The place seemed deserted, serene compared to its notoriety. We walked to where the "hole in the fence Pizza Hut" was supposed to be but it wasn't. After some exploration we found it a few blocks away then nestled down in the tall weeds to wait.

We let a few East bound trains pass, trains with only piggy-back cars and no cover. We wanted a train with 48 cars and enough room to hide. We debated whether we were being paranoid but after remembering the Chadwick cop's threat of 30 days in jail if caught within 10 days, we decided we were being "understandably cautious." So we waited.

All night it seemed, pickup trucks (maybe bulls, maybe workers..) appeared out of nowhere. Creeping silently then shining bright headlights in our direction. All we could do was freeze like deer on the highway and, like Sascha said already, "will ourselves invisible." Such a perfect description.

Our dream train arrived with dawn and we hopped on without incident, holding our breath all the way out of the yard. We though we were home free. Homeward bound. Then the train stopped.

Footsteps on the gravel. Crunch, crunch, crunch. Silence. Crunch, crunch, crunch. Silence. They must be checking the cars. Oh shit. Crunch, crunch, crunch. Right beside our car. Someone was climbing the ladder. OH SHIT!!

Curled up in the corners, we must have looked a strange sight to the man peering down at us. He looked startled, suprised to see us. "What's wrong with you?" he demanded of Dennis. "What's wrong with her?" he said motioning towards me. "Get up! Get up! Get up! Help me with this!"

It didn't take long to realize this was no bull. Nor was this a worker. This nervous man: sweaty forehead, bulging eyes, wielding three foot long bolt cutters, was here to rob the train. And he wanted our help.
"Get up! Get up! Get up!" he repeated loudly while mumbling something about making us rich.

No! Stay down! Stay down!" I whispered not wanting to get busted. Especially not as fucking accomplice to train robbery!

What's wrong with you? Get up and help me with this man!"
Dennis and I looked at each other with eyes wide. "What the fuck?!" was all I was thinking. (That's "What the fuck?" as in "this can't really be happening," or "are we dreaming?" Not as in "Hey - why not?")

But not knowing what else to do I watched, heart racing, as they went to work on the bolts. Crack! Off came one. Crack! Off came another. Crack! Off came the last. "Open the door! Come on man help me!" Mr. Train Robber was barking orders. They tried to pry it open, but before he could notice the top was still held together with wire, the train lurched forward. We all froze. Would he get off or would we have to? Should we anyway? And we're still in South Chicago, now living up to its reputation.

Too much of a pussy to say what I was thinking ("Get the FUCK OFF!!!"), I mustered up enough courage to say something along the lines of "Hey mister, the train's about to move. Are you gonna get off or what?" Mr. Train Robber replied with "Cool out baby" or some such shit. Then he gathered his crime tools and was gone.

We had only been stopped for a few minutes. It seemed like forever but at the same time it seemed like it didn't happen at all. We almost had to ask each other if it had been real. It was that weird. I mean think about it. Of all the cars**!!** On This damn long train - of all the cars...

Once again we were East bound. We laid low the whole ride, Justifiably Paranoid. But we were home free - slapping a special high five leaving Illinois. Then came night - sun down, no way to tell time or direction. No watch or compass. Straining to read highway signs or water towers. What did that say? Buffalo? New York? I didn't know we were supposed to go so far North (That's right - no train map either.) Are we headed for Canada? Where are we and what time is it? Someone said we'd be there by tonight. Who told you that? Hand-me-down information syndrome. I don't know where we are but we aren't where we need to be. Should we stay on? Or get off? Stay on..At least till morning so we know which direction we're headed. Come morning we found ourselves following the Hudson River South. Gorgeous. Even ventured out onto the "patio."

There's no way we could get busted here. Yeah. That's what we though in Chadwick, middle of nowhere cornfield town. OK. OK. Knock on wood. Three times. (Yes, I carry a piece of wood with me for just such occasions.) Breathtaking views. Morning on the Hudson.

We finally stopped near a cluster of soccer fields and exercise track and had to face the age old question yet again. Should we stay or should we go? The train was at a solid standstill, so we sat there for a while contemplating our position.

Finally we climbed down, reasoning that we could find out where we were in time to get back on if we had to. Looking pretty haggard and three shades of grimy, we brambled through the bushes and approached the nearest Mr. Fitness.
"Where are we?" we asked simply.
"You're in Teaneck, New Jersey."
"Oh. Where can we catch a bus or a train to NYC?"
"Right there," answered Mr. Fitness, pointing to a bench a few feet away, "comes every twenty minutes."

It was so perfect I laughed out loud. One hour later we were waking up at the end of the line - Port Authority Bus Terminal - New York City.

108

WRITE TO KATHY: 1822 LAMONT
WASHINGTON D.C. 20010

Dr. Scatter: We're staying in Montreal for a while. We were trying to mad dash across Canada to NewFieLand in 3 days to meet my friend. Hopping out of Toronto was impossible and we realized that without proper homage to GodMoney we wouldn't be able to catch the ferrie from Nova Scotia anyway. So, irritable ¿ desolute we started the trek out of the trainyard, up a steep hill. I stagered up, heavy pack pressing, uncomfortably on the base of my spine when I kicked a cardboard sign reading Montreal - 401 East. Well, there's no ignoring signs! And within an hour we caught a ride all the way here. The driver was a real circus performer, with the Cirque du Soliel Cool eh? I got a job the next day (same stuff) and made a hundred bucks yesterday, a small fortune to us now.

Pete is busy writing about his Arkansas experience and will send it to you soon. Our street fireshow duet has been a bomb here, we figure it works best during festivals as we did well in Toronto on Labour Day before running out of fuel. We heard of people doing shows in nightclubs here so we plan to modify and erotisize our haphazard routine to make it suitable indoors. Other than that we're attending vérnisage (art gallery openings) to enjoy wine ¿ cheese with the culture punks. I'm reading lots of George Orwell interesting notes on socialism ¿ poverty from P's friend Georgia's vast library. The dumpsters here awesome, cheese, fruit ¿ vegetables right across the road, fresh bread down the street and I'm learning to speak french! If u wanted 2 come up before heading south, just call: Angie's house:
(514) 2███████ is where we're staying, or call to say hi, whatever. Please say hi to the tribe in New York. for us. We both send our love to u. Thanx to your Mom
Love. Psycho Kitty, Mangily Lion ¿ Blue Dawg.
P.S. We'll still B in N.Y. early November.

THE AUTHOR ────────➤

MARTINE & PETER ARE CURRENTLY RESIDING AT C-SQUAT. THEY CAN BE REACHED AT: NY, NY P.O. BOX 20927 10009

"Whoa, check the giant pentagram!" Psychosomatic crouches excitedly in his seat. "I hear Texass has a lot of Satanists. Ai yai yoi yai yai!" Sticking his nugget out the window, he watches his rebel yell get stuck to the humid air.

Eyes flickering from the state's emblem to his friend's smashed-toothed grin, Mangily Lion swerves slightly, rig paw grabbing for the Connector Box. "Boogie Box to Red Thunder. What's your window?"

"We're in bleeping LogoLand waiting for you bleeping snail blazers!" The irate voice squawks at them through the ride's powerful speakers.

"Fuckin' fascist citizen band censorchips." Psycho Kitty hisses from her perch draped along the headrest of the last seat. The cat, uncharacteristically irritable following a week of embarrassing self inflicted accidents, scratches impatiently at her new rubber eye patch.

Blinded from her peripheral by the patch, pen poised over an endless letter to his lovegirl, MeganRella, Dr. Scatter glares across the ride at the arrogant cat. Jabbing his pen into a dark red vial of O-positive, he broods over hi words. Plop, drip, he grips his letter stick maliciously, squeezing out a juicy bubble of hemoglobin, permanently staining the ride's fur interior. *...narcissistic and glacier cold, rumored to be a free-range killer. I bet she'd just love to play fetc the vegan. What's a good adjective for a nasty feline?* Scribbling away furiously, Dr.Scatter describes his friends to MeganRella, covertly desiring an act of GodMoney to halt her band's x-continent blitz so she could re-join him and the Carnival of Caos. He drifts into the dimentions of making love on stilts.

> *Our father who aren't in heaven*
> *Surprise, surprise, the revolution's arrived*
> *Your kingdom's rust your will is dust*
> *On earth our lust is now our heaven*
> *Send us your kings, your cops, your Fascist pigs*
> *We can't forgive their trespasses*
> *We will serve them an equal lack of compassion*
> *The tables are turned-your guilt we burn*
> *While we suck cheesewhiz from your crosses*
> *For ours is the kingdom,*
> *The power and glory*
> *For ever and ever*
> *Jesus died for my entertainment!*

Mangily blasphemes loudly along with his own taped voice. Throngs of screaming teenage girls look up at him adoringly they heave against stage security--

"Hey, slow down, Mangily. Slow down!" Psychosomatic screeches into his ear hole, yanking him from the supe stadium concert venue of his mind.

"Shut-up, my tape's on!" Mangily roars.

"I don't drink shut-up. Serious, man. There's a stray, let's pick him up."

"A stray?" A voice curdles out of a pile on the floor. The pile scuttles up to the cockpit. Nugget Head 2, an inky photocopy of Nugget Head 1, pops up next to Psychosomatic poking him in the ear hole.

"Don't *even* touch me, Ditzy!" A sharp elbow to the rib-rack designed to barbeque her pop tarty impetuousness. Undaunted and notoriously opportunitarian, Ditzy sneaks a peek at the roadside diversion.

D.B.: *Highway silt swirls around your stomping feet, rising with each spin, engulfing you in its vortex. You undulate wildly, maniacally, arms twisting, fists flailing, imagining themselves smashing selfish drivers into the cheap fabric of thei empty passenger seats. Your hawk is plastered to your face, streaming green and purple rivers over your aching suncrisp body. Dance, you poor frustrated carless motherfucker and if no-one ever stops perhaps some benevolent god can spare a storm to drown you in.*

"Oh you got to pick him up. He's so cute, look at him wiggle." Ditzy giggles, straining against her nemesis, unwittingly usurping him from the coveted shotgun seat. Seething unbridled repugnance and irritation following months c poking, slapping, biting, teasing, giggling and any other form of girlie torture she could devise to steal his attention, the autocratic boy snaps. Psychosomatic slams SuperMouch against the ride's door. With an inhuman wail Ditzy's head eject through the open window portal hurtling directly at the stranded gypsy.

"Aspegma-brained, abortioned-faced, fetal-headed--" Thwack! Ditzy finally shut up by a stranger and a thirty mile per hour kiss.

The Underdawgs of the Boogie Box watch the hitcher jackknife and collapse with a nightmarish powerlessness. The filth of five thousand daily riders settles on the stunned heap o' hitcher.

D.B: *Well? Are you just going to lie there sucking up car manure? A ride finally stopped for you, ingrate. Better get off your asphalt before my gracious mood slides and they drive off leaving you stranded holding her head in your hands.*

An invisible vice fits around the his head sending a laser of pain to his frontal lobe, forcing his foggy eyes open with a pop. With two sharp twists of the head and an audible snap of the spine, the hitcher wobbles to his kryptonite shit kickers. Grabbing his licorice flavored travel bag, he boogies off toward the box.

"So you're just going to leave me rolling around? I⁴m the reason you're getting a ride at all--" A silver studded black leather hand shoves into the yammering. Silenced again, Ditzy.

Chomp, sharpened incisors sink into the tough worn leather hoping to disable the autograsp cable. *In vain,* the hitcher smirks to himself. *The brainless head obviously doesn't know about the new non-cable recycled leather self adhesive super grasper model no: 4080.*

Psychosomatic cheers as the hitcher nears the Box. He nudges Ditzy's limp grimy bod. "Want a little head?" He asks it sadistically as her face flies through the open window. Blurd, it lands in his lap, eyes up and staring at him defiantly from between his legs. A fluorescent gob horks out of the angry little face, splatting Psychosomatic between his red and black double irises. *Little Psycho four eyes,* Psychosomatic slips into Recall. Four words and the school badass stands rooted in horror. The red pupils dilate, separating long enough to complete an intense once over of the stocky bully. The obnoxious brat had just enough time to regret his words as his blood began to simmer his internal organs into a stringy pink pulp. Psychosomatic lingers on the initial guilty rush of allowing the intensity of his violent daydreams to overwhelm conscience. Gulping up a measure of focusing oxygen, he blots up the memory of the screaming leaky boy, squeezing it into a dormant file marked Ugly. He slides over to let the hitcher in.

"Whew cuz, I got to thank you for stopping. I felt like I was going to die there. I've been stuck there for three days." He slams the door behind him. Mangily winces, mentally assessing the ride's worn door latch assembly.

"I'll tell you one thing I learned about hitchhiking--is never do it in a place you can't walk out of." Psycho Kitty's ears perk at the questionable twang in the stranger's friendly drawl.

"Southern hospitality's a phrase the Yanks made up to cut deals with the Klansnecks." She eyes him coolly, yellow peppered greens unblinking.

"The name's Trevor Lution." He offers her the leather grip, tactically aware of her intention gauge yet unconcerned, shrugging off the mental mechanism as an outdated, unreliable pirate gimmick. Still uncertai, Psycho Kitty nods her greeting, keeping her paws to herself.

"Ahmmmmph" groans Psychosomatic's lap. Yanking the head up by its two inch purple strip, Psycho magnamiously reunites the two halves. Screwing the head into the neck attachment, he smoothes his fingers over the adhesive safety flaps. Exhausted and slightly embarrassed, Ditzy slinks past, expressionless, to fall into a heap in the rear corner of the ride. Dr. Scatter looks up from his letter long enough to smirk as she plops down beside him.

A rainbow of iridescent stars dances a spiral over the skin of the passengers. Trevor Lution looks up in awe. "That's awesome, cuz. I haven't seen one of those since epoch skipping on academy field trips." Straining his neck, he gazes into his own patched reflection in the chipped mirrors of an archaic disco ball. The funky sphere twists to a dizzying momentum forcing his eyes away.

"Oh that old piece of glass crap. Psycho Kitty picked it up when we squatted an abandoned kitcherie. I keep throwing it out but it seems to mysteriously re-attach itself to the ceiling." Mangily whips around to glare at his wife.

She yawns back. "I told you sixteen times that I didn't put it back there, although I'll hospitalize you if you toss it again. Now hurry up, they're waiting for us at LogoLand and I'm starving."

* * *

Bent Rock taps his fingers on the steering column relentlessly. The four passengers of Red Thunder sit sullen and cranky, waiting as usual for the other rides.

Shadow Hand creates fuzzy silhouettes on Bent Rock's chintzy seatback, against the dull glow of the solar reservoir street lamp. The scene is too familiar to him. The characters: aloof, unapproachable Firesnake, and DeBoner, his own suave, charismatic alter ego. The schmaltzy candlelight and table wine soundtrack plays in his head, he mouths the dialogue silently. A firefly from a bottle in his pocket becomes a prop. Firesnake coils around herself alluringly. She dances with the fly seductively, eating it, then letting it flutter out again. She teases it, blowing it brighter and brighter as it suspends like magic, inches above her head. She stretches up, reaching above her head to caress her brilliant plaything. Shadow Hand shivers at her uncharacteristic tenderness. DeBoner swaggers in, attracted, eager and cock-sure of himself.

"Hey Firesnake, want to go to the smutfest with me tonight?" *Direct, with a friendly inquiring tone. A solid approach, at least two technique points there,* he gloats.

Abruptly extinguishing the gentile firefly, Firesnake expands alarmingly until she towers over him, easily three times his size. A mouth the size of his head snaps open.

"STOP SMOTHERING ME!"

Shadow's hands fall to his lap in dismay. Like a nightmare or a bad LSD trip he always becomes a mere character in his own shadow plays, unable to direct a more satisfying outcome. He peeks through a matty curtain of unwashed hair at the real Firesnake, staring petulantly out the window, open sketchbook in her lap. He gazes at her hungrily, wondering if life would imitate art if he could muster the self confidence to get in control of his fantasy icons.

Wrapped up in a cloak of solitude, stinking of people repellent, Lizard Boy sits one seat behind Shadow Hand craving a drink. *Nobody understands*, he bitches to himself. *Why don't you just stop drinking? They ask like it was that fucking simple. That's like telling a manic depressant to just cheer up.* His body convulses on a dry heave. He settles back into his seat, placating himself on the chance of an unevaporated puddle of acid rain mix lying around LogoLand.

Firesnake stares out the window, pen doodling paper formlessly. Her thoughts drift between the elusive warrior wanna-b design her friends are expecting and her present boy overload. She directs her attention to the more overwhelming of the two dillemmas. Her gaze flits between Tutu, her latest acquisition, sitting shotgun and looking luscious, and Shadow Hand despondently playing with himself. She wonders what the hell she's going to do when they all meet up with her third yet favorite fuckthing who might show up anytime, anywhere along the way.

D.B.: *Yeah, and I'm looking in the mirror all the time, studying what they all see in me. I've been funny, I've been cool with the lines. Ain't that the way love's supposed to be?*

*   *   *

"Now we've lost everybody." Mizz T exasperates from the rear of the Cohesive Mobile. "I told you caravaning was a stupid idea."

Beside her, Beatmaster lowers his head, hands flying over the synthiskin of the ride's built in mini metal harmony center.

"Actually, we haven't." Super Bra bounces up, fresh from a nap in a D cup. "The Silver Slut is still right on our ass and I can see LogoLand at twelve o'clock."

Peeler grips the steering column, exhausted after two straight days of navigating. Her brain throbs in time with the unrelenting triple quarter beat.

"Complainers on eject! Complainers on eject!" Peeler hollers at the backseat. "So shut the fuck up about caravaning."

Super Bra, stiff with the tension, whistles low into the imposed silence.

"Was that a peep?" Peeler pivots her ears into the unaccustomed noislessness.

"I can say whatever I want." Tiny yet audible, Mizz T chants her empowering mantra all the way to LogoLand.

*   *   *

Pimp Slap steers the Silver Slut into an available slot, silently grumbling the disadvantages of caravaning so incohesively. "I don't see the Boogie Box anywhere." She complains to the herd layered into the backseat of her cramped whore machine.

"I hope they weren't ordered off the travelway again. I thought I saw a donut inhaler back there and Mangily still doesn't have a ride permit." Esssa steps out allowing Tee Flee, Catfish, Baba, Ghia, Android, Hara and Sari, Virgin and Nivirg, Kiem, Odi-O, Low Key, Poetrix and Poli Fuckie to pile out of the Slut.

"Holy fishburger!" Whiskers rising to the occasion, Catfish surveys a veritable sea of dumpsters. Row upon row of shiny clean fast food receptacles, each proudly brandishing its own colorful fast food logo. Parched mouths water in unison, eyes scanning favorite labels: Taco Bile, Karcass King, Subspew, Gardies, Pizza Pig, Diarrhea Queen, McDumpys...

"It really does exist!" The Cohesives run over excitedly. Peeler left behind to secure the ride. One can never be too sure in these desolate corporate minefields. The PSA (Psycho Scavengers of America) have been known to squat under dumpsters, sawing holes in the floor to gobble up the waste directly from the chute. Peeler, a unit of the universe, knows about such things. Keeping a sharp eye on the waste disposal units, she wanders over to join the group.

The Underdawgs present mob around Bent Rock and Lizard Boy to hear the tales of disappointment first hand.

"I've never seen anything like it before, the locks are kryptonite or something, I stuck my survival knife in it and it melted." Rock holds up a charred handle looking around the group uneasily.

"Naw. I keep telling ya, it's that newfangled laser pin. Some PSA guy told me about them a while ago. Some kind of Block aided Starve the Cretin campaign." Lizard Boy takes a swig from the stale bottle of Liquid Paradise he scored out of the ditch.

D.B.: *Of course the Block is playing trix on you dumpster diving dimwits. But not quite so obvious. It's a mirage. Those gleaming dumpsters are all compactors!*

Poetrix turns to Android. "Did you just say something?"

"Negative."

"It sounded like," she thinks for a moment, "compactors."

"I hope not, that would really suck." Tee Flee, having recently lost her magic tief box to a donut inhaler, runs a small hand over her concave tummy. Baba, Esssa and Rock jog over to the structure in question.

"I could kill a cow for a hamburger right about now." Esssa complains to no-one in particular.

Baba drums a positive vibe over the McDumpy's logo.. "When we get this open, you can have all the hormone puppies you can cram in."

Head tilted, Rock squints into the lock mechanism. A thin sliver of blue light connects the two layered lids to the cupboard units. "Lizard Boy was right, it is a laser pin." Rock thinks hard. "Shadow!" He calls to Red Thunder.

Lurking off between Pizza Pig and Taco Bile, Shadow Hand feels the voice tugging at his body as his name is called. "Jeez, no need to be so insistent," he yells at his friend as he floats, still pulled by the voice. Plopping down between Baba and Esssa, Shadow glares at Rock. "That system's very inconvenient, not to mention unbalanced."

"Is it really fair? Is any of it really fair?" Baba teases Shadow the Unbalanced Grump.

Esssa whines, clutching her stomach. Rock's attention remains fixated on the laser lock. "Hey Shadow, you know some kind of trick for this kind of lock, doncha?" He moves his hand toward the laser. Shadow shrieks warning Rock to withdraw his hand.

"The intensity of the blue light will sear right through flesh. It's designed with you blood dependent creatures in mind." His smug, if slightly racist tone does not escape Baba's judgment. Shadow plunges a translucent hand into the mechanism. "My father had one of these on his virtual sex stimulator until I forgot to turn the lights off one night. Otherwise he would have never figured it out. He was blood dependent too." *That's it*, Baba thinks to himself, *he's definitely racist. These see through types always thing they're better than everybody.*

"I like to think of myself as bloody cool, thank-you." Baba's most vehement mock British in his face.

Shadow, picking up the defensive tone, retaliates as an Aussie. "What are the two most common elements in the universe, mates?" No response. "Hydrogen and stupidity. Now we all got something in common, eh?" Baba smirks., *most common elements to your ego maybe.*

Tension broken, the three b-types watch Shadow's Hand envelope the tiny blue staff. *1 Firesnake, 2 Firesnake, 3 Firesnakes*, he counts under his breath. The heavy lids suddenly spring up to fall open on its hinges. They crowd around to peer into the container. A tidal wave of disappointment ebbs through their cavernous stomachs.

"It is a compactor," someone murmurs. They look at the mulch of a hundred leftover dinners and try not to cry.

D.B. :*Activate lightbulb.*

Rock, propelled by an unfamiliar force, jogs around the bin. "Hey guys, this bulge here has a separate lid, maybe 's some kind of feeder bin." Shadow glides around to apply his expertise on the second lock. *1 Firesnake, 2 Firesnakes, 3 Firesnakes*...and ...bang, another lid clanks open. Shadow Hand congratulates himself with an invisible pat on the back as Esssa dives into a sea of burgers. Bingo.

"Hamburgers, cheeseburgers, bacon double cheeseburgers, bacon triple cheeseburgers, oh my lard, I'm in heaven!" Esssa shrieks deliriously, tossing packaged meat to the three non-flesh eaters.

Android, a non-eater, trundles over. " Mock Flesh has a bin in the corner for you veganites." He offers helpfully. A shrill b movie hair raising scream comes from the bin.

"Something's got a hold of my wrist!" Esssa screams again. Rock grabs at her legs while Baba and Shadow jump up to scan the interior. Esssa howls hysterically at her arm which appears painfully positioned, hand submerged in the swamp of meat.

"Esssa calm down!" Rock yells up at her frantically. "Is the thing you're caught on sharp? I mean, am I going to rip you're hand off if I tug at your legs?"

"I don't know," the words barely strangle through her lips as Rock heaves mightily on her legs. Her hand emerges through the burgers. Attached to her wrist is a big red glove. Attached to the glove is a long golden arm. A man rises from the burger patch.

Esssa shrieks uncontrollably. The Underdawgs of the three rides converge in horror. The big red glove relaxes its grip. Esssa snaps back wards into Rock's arms. Ghia and Poli Fuckie bark excitedly.

"Caught ya. Trix aren't for kids, they're for corporations." The two giant cherry red lips wobble unsteadily as he speaks. "Silly brats. "

Wait, was that a lick of fire between his lips? Firesnake locks her gaze on his mouth.

"Trick or treat!" Baba 's relief receives a few nervous giggles.

"What the hell are you supposed to be, dumpster patrol?" Tee Flee quizzes the clown.

"That's one of my duties, yes. I'm the McEmployee of the Month." His neon red afro rises toward the sky displaying an electronic message board sewn into his golden uniform. The title McEmloyee of the Month scrolls endlessly across his chest.

113

"Aw come on, we're really hungry," Catfish whines, "Can't you let us have just a few McRocks? You're just going to pulverize them anyway."

Super Bra leans toward him, "Yeah, we wont tell Ronald."

"Show some respect!" The twisted mouth barks at them. "Ronald McDumpy was our founding forefather and h is directly responsible for the freedoms you cherish today. It's upon his McRocks that the United States of McDumpys w built. He was the original Colonial Corporate Capitalist."

"It's simple economics, Mister. You have excess supply." *Mabey logic will twist his lock,* Low Key reasons to himself.

"Economics my ignorant little sycophant, involves the trade, exchange and accumulation of GodMoney." The letters on his Personnal Message board melt and fuse into GodMoney. He spits at them distastefully. "Heathens."

"You're going to live your whole life slaving away for a greedy green symbol? Odi-O can't fathom the point.

"GodMoney dosen't care who your parents were, GodMoney dosen't care what colour you are, GodMoney dosen' care who your girlfriend is--"

"GodMoney dosen't care about you!" The corner of Kiem's mouth tics up, unacostomed to the vehemence of the voice coming out of it. The corner of the giant's grusome mouth tics down, outraged at such a rude interuption.

"Yeah, It's not about GodMoney, it's about your pathetic life. GodMoney doesn't even know you exist." Hara glares up at him fiercely.

The facsist clown looks incredulous. "I have Billions Serving GodMoney 24-7! The Law of Fiscal Order ensure that I will get what I deserve!" The giant elasticized body snaps back and forth violently. The message now reads Billior Serve.

Peeler, sick of all the BS, spies an opportunity, winking at Tee Flee and Catfish. Peeler moves closer to the McEmployee of the Month. The Underdawgs wonder what her plan could be as she begins to gyrate her hips furiously. Mizz T nods her comprehension to Super Bra and together they chant ancient incantations, clapping and stomping out tribal rhythms. Beatmaster joins in, belting a hypnotic tattoo out of a pocket beat wand. The clown appears bemused by spectacle.

Peeler grabs a hold of her hair, one long plait in each hand. The Underdawgs watch on in fascination as slowly, seductively, she undresses the first layer of epidermis from her face. She flips, she swirls, she pirouettes, facial skin peele to the base of the spine, slapping against her collar bone. Pimp Slap, returning from paradise a little too late the night

before, stifles a retch. Peeler moans guttural sexulation. Grabbing the next two layers at once, she exfoliates herself raw, smiling groovegastically. That's it for Pimp Slap, who turns away to puke in a quiet, neat, polite puddle.

McFreak of the Week, apparently enjoying himself, claps his gruesome red mitts together. Without warning, he plunges a monstrous paw back into the burger bin. His eyes glitter dollar signs in triumph as his fingers emerge wrapped around Tee Flee. The respected Tief stands rooted to his palm in shock, a stack of evidence in either hand, fries and pies spilling out of her pockets. Peeler screams her bloody head off and the music stops.

Lifting her level to his hollow eyes, he squints at her maliciously. "There's only one thing lower than a kid with no cash and that's a dumpster tief." Just as Tee Flee opens her mouth to defend herself, a burger, the density of a stone, shoots out of the clown's mouth, banging her on the temple. Tee Flee collapses out of his hand, unconscious. Android speeds to her aid, catching her limpness heroically, seconds before kissing the cement. He rushes his friend to the safety a distant dumpster.

The clown smiles sadistically. The flames of his charcoal broiled heart play around his lips as two more petrified Big Smacks shoot from his oral cannon in instant succession. "Smiles are free. Enjoy your meal and have a nice day!!!" He rants at his audience.

Firesnake, mesmerized by his evil flames gets clipped square on the forehead. She falls backward into Tutu's arms. He drags her behind the nearest container.

*　　*　　*

D.B.: *Lights, Music, Action. Call off your army, familyfucker. Take back your assorted wingnuts. Take back your Frenc! Flies, your Chicken McNugget Heads, your corrupt McCheesy Burgler. Take back Grim before he gets maced. I'm coming to stain your uniforms, fuck up your orders and tear your McHappy place mats to shreds.*

Lights on full illumination, disco music rattling the ride's powerful speakers, the Boogie Box finally pulls into LogoLand. A scene of chaos has boiled up between the tidy rows of dumpsters. The late arrivals stare on in disbelief. A giant hysterical clown growing out of a dumpster pelts their friends with McDumpy's products. An electric message loope across his chest flashes: *Big Smack, fillet of flesh, quarterpounder, french flies, icy cock, thick Snakes, sundays and apple spies. You deserve to break today*— Lizard Boy grins as he shuts the corporate spew up with a quarter pounder to the hear

D.B.: *Don't just stand there bovine, mooove! Go save your friends! Or have all the warriors turned to worriers?*

The side door of the Boogie Box slides open unaided. The ride dims its own I-beams as the music continues to mp through the speakers. The Disco Ball begins to spin, mirrors polished to a gleam. Picking up momentum, working f loose, the great ball floats over the gaping dawgs to freedom outside the Box. Feeling stunned yet pushed into motion ome inexplicable force, the dawgs file out after the ball.

Trevor is the fist to feel it. A familiar twitch in his legs and arms, the disco music infused in his blood causing his rt to beat in double time. "This is it!" He yells at the dawgs, "the Trevor Lution has arrived." The delirious hitcher ms to dance.

Psycho Kitty, not so sure about any Trevor Lution but never missing an opportunity to boogie down, grabs Dr. tter, the two jumping onto the lid of the nearest compactor.

B.: *Everybody up off the floor, the dawgs are going to boogie-oogie-oogei 'til they just can't boogie no more.*

Magically infused with the spirit of dance and play, the warring Underdawgs drop their ammo to join the promptu party. Tee Flee snapping back to consciousness in the nick of time, springs off the ground, executing a perfect rial over the Karcass King container. Tutu, eager to join the festivities, gently slaps the still unconscious Firesnake.

The giant fascist abruptly stops flinging the nasty burgers, arms dropping to his side helplessly, his attention terly transfixed on the rotating disco ball. The clown stars hard at the funky sphere as it rises to eye level. All the greed d lovelessness of the controller's empty life reflects in it's thousand little mirrors. The gaudy green money symbols from e monster's irises cascade toxic iridescence over LogoLand.

"GodMoney" the clown gasps, "I knew you would come."

"Yes" the great and powerful voice of D.B. resonates through the dancers. "And now I'm going to rescue you om your horrible empty controlled existence." With that the disco ball spins 360 around the clown's head. The clown, antic not to lose sight of its deity, twists revolution after revolution until it's cap is good and childproof. The hideous

own squeals uncomfortably, the extra intake of oxygen just the pressure necessary for a bottled explosion. Deflated, the olden uniform crumples to a heap. The grotesque head plummets into the container, the lid banging shut with the force.

"Ding dong, the wicked clown is dead." Psychosomatic dances around McDumpy's container.

His deed of the day done like dumpsterd dinner, D.B. modestly speeds back to his home in the Boogie Box. Free f their oppression, the lids of LogoLand spring up all around the exhausted, starving dancers. The Underdawgs scramble ff to dive into the bin of their favorite toxins.

Firesnake blinks into consciousness. Psycho Kitty, Mangily Lion, Dr. Scatter, Poetrix and Baba crowd around her. I had the strangest dream," she slurs, groggy, "we killed convention and we were disco dancing on his grave while some ig hunk of glass flew around over our heads." Grabbing a handful of cold soggy fries she traces a design on the asphalt f LogoLand:

-Martine-

Author's Note: Please understand that while the characters in the story were initially based upon the people i met last summer, i took so much liscence in writing fiction that they all evolved into their own monsterous entitys. My pen eloped with a nightmare to procreate a smelly knot of paper frankensticns.

No offence was intended to anyone!.!. And no, my disco ball didn't tell me to say that.

-M.S.-

thinking wicked thoughts about the FUTURE

So what we did last Summer was an experiment. A kind of fucked up experi
where all the scientists were drunk when the results were coming in, by
experiment nonetheless..Here's my thoughts on what some of our mistakes
and how things could be done better in the future:

1) The fixed schedule thing really screwed us up in the end: it threw us
unwillingly right into the center of the beast. If you're going to live on
capital time - you need <u>capital</u>! We were broke(stupid word) and there were
lot of us and we always seemed to gravitate towards the market place - the
strip(there's one in every town.) Organizing our route around urban centers
perpetuated that whole dynamic, but let's face it: despite a small minority
we're city scavengers. We're urban parasites. We know how to scam and hustl
and live out of the wastes of the city. Don't put us out in the middle of t
woods because we wouldn't know what the fuck to do with ourselves! Sad but
I'm opening up a dumpstered can of worms here, so before I go off on a mill
tangents let me get to my first point -
Don't set up a week by week schedule with people around the country if you
have any money! Straight up. We wasted more of our energy last summer tryin
figure out how we were going to pay for gas..we stripped the copper out of
abandoned buildings and sold them to scrap yards - we scammed food stamps i
every town, any kind of cool symbiosis we would have created with our audie
when we did street theater it seemed to get lost in a scramble ms for solic
(in my opinion^{ATLEAST}- that's up for discussionxxxxx I guess) We scraped by and
OK, but it left us without much to put back into the communities we were gu
because our energy was so low.

2) Alright, this is just an idea, but I for one would be very interested in
seeing/helping to organize some kind of urban/rural @ gathering out on some
somewhere - ideas can be exchanged(because we definately have much to lear
from each other} - networks between farming collectives and urban food
collectives can be bridged - us city folk can learn to be more autonomous b
growing our own food and building shelters - rather than always tapping in
the infrastucture that we all know isn't always going to be around. Maybe w
can teach you to dumpster dive and squat and hop trains - I don't know...

3) The Nomadic Festival suffered seriously from XXXXXXXXX a lack of concre
unifing projects we could all work on together.A More organized street thea
Project would have done the trick - more planning from the outset obviously
would have given us a base to work from rather than patching everything
together at the last second. Ikept having the feeling last Summer that we
were spreading ourselves too thin - that we would have got a lot more accomp
if either a) we had stuck to one or two projects and perfected them or b)if
had been in smaller groups that converged at key times but each worked on t
own projects.(i.e. a billboard crew and a theater crew or whatever..)

4)I think some kind of future traveling project would be wise to plan actions and events a) in smaller towns or even suburbs, where the flow of radical information is virtualy nil and a whole bunch of anarchist freaks could really blow some minds and open some eyes b)maybe weaving and centering around colleges and universities where the future leaders and business folk get their ways set in them - it's so important to show people that there really are different ways to live and survive and expose people to alternatives (campuses are also the ideal places to gather supplies and resources and money!) Just following XXX our normal migration patterns and sticking to the travelers circuit made it kind of useless to spread radical information because a lot of times it would have just been preaching to the converted.

5) Utilizing communication technology. Us @ folks have to get our shit together. Relying on the postal service unless we have some super scam going is a waste of money and paper (I cringe when I think about the hell if I'm about to go through trying to distribute this monstrosity..) The phone lines most of us have down pretty well,but it seems to me that the Internet could be agreat tool for networking if it was used properly. I know it's going on but I guess I'm stuck in the past or something. A quick way to distribute information to a lot of people everywhere for cheap sounds pretty good to me.If ALL the @ bookstores and cafes and pieces of land and collectives were hooked up on line around the country (world!) we'd be doing pretty well.//There's a thriving new movement of pirate radio stations creeping up all over this country which is totally exciting. Here in NYC we've been broadcasting every Friday for about two months now - no stable space so we've been floating around all the squats like a TAZ party and it's been a magnet for talented artists and musicians and poets from our community. There has been a lot of discussion going on, mostly inspired by the stuff taking place in the Bay Area of California, regarding the set up of some type of pirate radio alliance or underground associated press which I think would be a worthing project indeed. While we were on the road last Summer, I was calling up Free Radio Berkeley every week and giving them live on the air updates to our progress which on a bigger scale would be great for some kind of traveling band of nomads.

6)Finally, I'd like to thank everyone whox in any way put us up last summer or had a hand in feeding or suppprting our crew. We were totally winging it and dispite any fuck ups or people we might have alienated: our intensions were good! I hope in the future that if more projects like this take off, the folks doing the organizing keep this stuff in mind: provide shelter for your sorry asses (whether it be tentxx large tents or prearranged housing or whatever) so you don't end up having to leach off your friends. The same goes for food: a ki makeshift kitchen set-up would have helped us out enormously not only because it would have kept us from always trying to find houses to cook in, but it also would have provided a means and excuse to gather and work togehher. Without a doubt, always have something to give back to the places you stay - whether it be in the form of gifts or spiritual inspiration - it don't matter - respect for peoples spaces and clans is xxx so important - cause everything that you do, good or bad, comes back around later and either taps you on the shoulder or smacks you in the head, respectively.

So that's what I gotta say..

DR. SCATTER
IN THE EARLY HOURS..

An increasing influx of nomads and nomadic groups, overlapping and coordinating, at times for major focusses, remains potent with promises of pleasure and subversion. I travelled with a group in a school bus this summer. We were on a paralell course with the Nomadic Festival -- but there hasn't been as much communication and cross-fertilization as there might be. I wonder what others feel they've learned from this summer's travels; how did things go differently than envisioned, and would you do it different next time? Are people thinking about a next time? I know I am.

I know some people who are already organizing for a caravan next summer with eight major stops accross the country, they hope will attract around 2,000 people. It's to be a grand alliance, "bringing together the punks and the dead heads," etc. Although I really like the people who are doing this, I didn't even think it was a great idea to shoot for 100 people travelling together, as Arrow envisioned for the Nomadic Festival. And while people overcoming stereotypes and sectarianism is excellent, I'm not sure bringing people together on the basis of acceptance of stereotypes is the best way to do it. Some people may be trying to model a nomad scene here on what's happenned in England, where, I hear, there's been huge gatherings of like 30,000 people suddenly showing up in a rural area, which really has been out of control in some beautiful ways and definitely caused problems for the authorities. So maybe we'll have that here -- but it may be that the best strategy is to focus on the small group, the <u>band</u> of nomads, the pack of wolves, whatever size is best for maximum autonomy expansion and anarchy-fomenting potential. And dare to do it not for the spectacle you can make of an externalized festival, but for the liberation of making a festival of your life.

I've seen glimpses of strange (not easily named / defined / controlled) actions breaking through barriers and engaging and seducing unsuspected people to participate, to dance and go mad on a street corner in a small city, beffuddled police standing by perplexed. So I want to extend in that direction of achieving a palpably different quality of experience, challenging your self and an environment, pushing the psycho-geographical pressure points that mold and restrict behavior in spaces. So many people get stuck revelling in the appearance of rebellion! Consider the idea that energy put toward looking weird can take away from energy put toward actually being weird.

Let's not settle for a shallow notion of festivity, play, and the subversiveness of fun. To me, week-by-week scheduling indicates that. Why not shoot for creating a zone of festivity and conviviality that could really engage a place -- and that means maximum flexibility, awareness of constraints, and deadly accurate spontanaeity. Stay in a place for a month if things really get rolling, doing lawn-rip-ups for free feast gardens, anti-school book-mobile day at the local junior-high, and other interventions into "official culture," as well as totally gratuitous festalness. That's what I wanted to do this summer. Much of it remains to be realized, awaiting the right mix of ingredients, people, and energies. The Nomadic Festival is Dead! Long Live Nomadic Festivity!

Contacts:

UnruLEE
4743 Hiawatha AV.S#116
Mnpls., MN 55406

Sasha K.
41 Sutter St. Suite 1661
S.F., CA 94101

Well Sascha's been on my ass to write something for the zine for about three months now, and since he's taking it to the printer tomorrow I guess this is it!- -> The Nomadic Festival is an idea that has existed for a long time. It's an idea that's been floating freely in the consciousness and casual conversions of American radicals for many years now - each with their own variations and ideas, twists and spices.

So, as I plucked this idea from the psychic network of the waste-nations refuse and began to literate it into some kind of definitive plan, I started to realize what a great opportunity this would be to define and explore radical politics within some of our North American sub-cultures. If nothing else, it would be a good forum for communications and networking with different groups and individuals. Being recently inspired by Hakim Bey and other writers, I hoped that the Nom Fest could explore forms of poetic terrorism and creative culture stimulation as well as become a catalyst for radical organizations and eventually be used as a foundation for alternative, non-taxable economy (i.e. barter fairs, etc.)

Well, the response was good and the ideas were many, but the Nomadic Festival was about more than just ideas - it was about action!

Yes, we would soon attempt to straddle the gaping chasm between rampant ideology and manic activity.

The 13th Street evictions went down, as time sped up, and my inner voice blasted a trumpet and announced: "On your mark...get set...Go!" My nomadic summer flew by in a flash and a blur. Hopefully you've gotten your fill of the sordid details in the rest of the magizine; I just want to reflect a bit about some of the goals and whether or not I feel we achieved them.

Goal #1 - To have a big traveling party during the summer of '95. Definitely achieved. Partying was certainly something we nomads didn't have a problem with last summer. In fact, we sometimes took flak for doing a bit too much of it. And many times, the question of partying vs. politics would come up, and the spirit of the reaction was: "Fuck Politics!" or "Partying is politics!" Who is it that said: "If I can't dance, I don't want your revolution."?

Speaking of politics, I really want to thank the good folks at Autonomedia for giving us support and I whole a lot of great books to take along. The book and 'zine distrbution was definitely one of my favorite aspects of the trip. Not only did it earn us a little cash when we were in a pinch, but it created a wonderful forum for discourse, communication, and education. I remember "working the tables" in Austin and what a great space for conversation it created in the midst of the punk-industrial-tribal rock mayhem of the warehouse. People would come up with poems or rants or zines they had done and want to talk about it. Or maybe they'd pick up one of our books that they had read previously and tell me all about it. I definitely consider the info. distro. a success and would encourage future traveling groups to try it.

Another goal was to have crazy days filled with workshops and information and every weekend filled with wild nights of music, poetry, performance, and creativity. This was somewhat successful, especially in places where there was a lot of local stuff organized already. In my original vision, the Nom Fest crew would have been more prepared with performance type entertainment material from the onset, (i.e. solo acts) and/or we would have had time to rehearse some kind of group performances. Well, the reality was that, although we had a lot of talent, none of us really were stage performers and we were all so frazzled from the squat evictions and getting ready to leave, that when we got to Philly and the weekend came around, we were looking at each other like "What now? What are we going to do?" Well, I guess you'll get the details of what happened elsewhere in the zine, but the point is, we were in a constant state of trying to figure out all that stuff as we went along. We were constantly trying to consolidate our talents and create our Carnival of Chaos theater, but it was always very difficult. We were nomads, travelers. We knew the road and how to get by on it, but now we were trying to be some kind of traveling theater group, something we definitely weren't used to. Rehersals were nearly impossible as someone would always be off drinking, or shoplifting, or scamming gas money for the trip. Then there was also the question of stages. We had a lot of discussion on how stages tend to create such a barrier between the performer and the audience and we talked a lot about how we could avoid that problem. We were always trying to pick up new talents and perfect old ones, and, I think, we patched together some pretty good performances last summer. But more often than not, we were the ones raising hell and partying below the stage rather than standing on it.

A larger, more theoretical goal, was to help lay a foundation for a new sub-culture. That is, the quest to break down the isolation barriers and begin to set in motion new social (r)evolutions. Or, as I wrote in the first Nom Fest zine: "the idea of this event is to create radical, anti-capitalist, multi-cultural, sustainable networks to help our peoples' free themselves from our repressive society." Quite a lofty goal: to steal the politics of our bloated yet starving society and forge it into new ideology and action for the future. I feel that if I asked anyone involved with the Nomadic Festival: "Did we start a new movement?" they would probably laugh at me. But, anyone who travels in, networks with, or is involved in the radical movements today, might agree that "Nomadic Festivity" (as Unrulee puts it) has a valuable role to play in our struggles.

Well, the next question you might ask is: "what is that role?" It's definitely something we talked about as we traveled together last summer. What does a group of traveling nomads have to offer the underground networks or a better society? Well, a few things I think.. One is news and information. What they saw in the last town, and the town before that, and what impression they have of the whole area they traveled through. One who travels a lot tends to have a more objective perspective towards the "big picture." We do have lots of other access to news and info via zines, telephones, and the internet, but some would argue that nothing can replace a good old face to face conversation. Another obvious service nomadic groups might provide could be the distribution of goods. Nomad could easily avoid unsavory or unfair tarrifs and regulations by moving goods from one area to another. I'm sure I could think of many benefits that nomads could and do bestow, but I feel the most important that we have to offer is inspiration, vitality, and excitment. Just as a body of water that does not move becomes stagnant, we see communitites that have little or no flow of people become dull and boring. Closed communities can become isolated and even xenophobic because of lack of activity. On the contrary, somewhere like New York or San Francisco are great examples of places that have a constant influx of people from all over the world and thrive. Culturally speaking, these places provide people with inspiration and a heightened sense of tolerance. We nomads can provide people with that inspiration. To dance, to sing, to stay up all night and alter billboards, whatever. We don't have to get up and go to work in the morning, this *is* our job. To have fun, to stir up trouble, to throw a party in the middle of town or in the middle of nowhere. If you really like what we're doing, you can quit your job and join us. "Drop out and join the Circus!" was last summers battle cry,(well besides "got an extra cigarette? or "spare some change?")So anyway, the point I'm trying to make is that the Nomadic Festival was a great thing and although the Nom Fest '95 is over I hope that the idea of the Nomadic Festival can continue to blossom and thrive. Start networking now to set up your activities for the summer, and remember, when you're pissed or frustrated by this fucked-up system, don't bitch - create alternatives!!

See you on the road!

THE PARADE OF ALIEN REDEMPTION MARCHES INTO THE NEW MILLENIUM

by sp@m

One of the greatest days in my life was my last day in Berkeley where I had been staying for the past three weeks. I had come to the Bay area for the Food not Bombs international gathering which were glorious days!!! Sneaking food past riot cops, meeting people from all over the country, and getting arrested three mondays in a row.

After a brief trip up North I found myself spending three weeks in Berkeley waiting for the Nomadic festival and trying to get out of a severe funk. I'd been staying in the east bay instead of San Francisco because it was easier to get around and I wanted to meet up with the Nomadic Festival

Plans of escaping to Arcata with Andrew had fallen apart and I had felt my brain turn mushy like a table dived salad from cafe intermezzo with too much dressing. Things had begun to look up the week of born of fire with Marcus's back yard full of people making me feel less lonely. A whole bunch of us had gone to the beach in Tim's van allowing the freezing cold water to shock me out out of my depression and loneliness which had kept me from enjoying most of the born of fire workshops.

about a month before, I had been talking to somebody at the black maggot house about born of fire. He told me about the mud people who annually walk around financial or shopping districts covered only in mud. It sounded like the culmination of a lot of ideas I'd been thinking about a long time I hadn't done political stuff before FNB because I had always seen political shit as symptoms of a dark cultural undercurrent. As I began to delve into the network of travelers, public art, punk shows, graffiti, squatting, dumpster diving, etc: I noticed how far away I had always been from most peoples realities even when I'd been trapped in their excuse for a culture. Finding more people with similar ideas has led me to feel like we're from another planet,

121

invaded and colonized in the womb by the shopping mall t.v. aliens of Planet Commodidty and held in chains and degrading stares for the rest of our lives.

But, what of our invasion? When would the wing-nuttians dive bomb the invader's bubble, bursting it open to drip away like kudzu takes over a highway? Mud people and the parade it was part of was such an invasion.

The parade was talked about beforehand, mostly as a protest against consumerism, but beyond "ism" anticonsumerism is really about being alive and being human-not commodity....it is also about having more fun than can be imagined in advertising reality. The parade was an explosion in the face of the dull routine of Saturday shoppers & cars rolling silently into the planet's death. However, at first it was just us sitting around in Ho Chi Minh park awkwardly waiting for something to happen. some people showed up in traditional anarchist protest black. Marcus broke out his Crass stencil and we did my shirt that I wore most of the summer. I was wearing shorts which I felt uncomfortable in wondering if the mud people were going to show up. One of Marcus's housemates was nervous about the mud people and clothing now that public nudity laws had changed in Berkeley. I stood there feeling the body weirdness humiliation feeling that I'd been programmed into.

All of a sudden, the van pulled up and Arrow and the Shadow Puppet Guy began unloading the costume trunks. More peopel started showing up wearing makeup and masks from the week before. Strange clothes began tossing around. People got up on stilts. Tatyana had purple spirals on her face as she towered high and mighty. There was a big banner that read "Buy Bye America". I found a piece of net-like black cloth that I could see through and wrapped it around my head. I went and sat with some of the people from Texas I'd been hanging out with. Some of us would become Los Vagabundos Pirate Crew later that night, dubbed so by Aaron after 48 hours of good shoplifting luck, which I was too chicken to take part in.

One of the guys, who was digging into his first 40oz. of the day looked at me and said, half sarchastic and half as a dare, "you should go stick your head in the soup." Inspired, I grabbed a 2nd helping of congealed bean stew into a cup and smeared it over my black shroud entwined' head. Then Kadon (not correct spelling) got a bucket for water, and someone else jumped the fence to get dirt. Mud happens first to those who make it happen. Four of us removed our clothes and rolled in the puddle of cold black ooze. It dried in the sun leaving us sheathed in new skin. I stood triumphant with a round headpad of vomitous stewed black cloth and mud of naked regal. It even grossed some of the nomad's out. Banners, masks, Mud, stilts, drums, noise....We hit Telegraph screaming en masse through the parking lot of the Yuppie supermarket, a fierce wave of human wingnut power enveloping. We reached the main drag and shoppers stood pointing and gawking. I remember old men laughing. People ran around passing out pamphlets that looked like strange dollar bills. Cameras were everywhere. I have never had so many pictures taken of me and I still have not seen a single one of them from that day.

Tightened rubber riot cops lined the university entrance witht he blank stare of discomfort. We turned the corner and walked down past the line laughing. we rounded Shattuck Ave and blocked the cars heading through their slow crawl. the cop vehicles came closer and someone got arrested for going too near a diner, but we kept on.

Eventually the energy died down and we mudpeople draped ourselves with what we could find. I took off my new head. The cops followed us back to the park adn hung out for awhile watching us and taking down the tag numbers of the vans. As we wandered toward the Chateau to beg showers, a cop turned to the mudpeople and said in the tone of an angry parent, "How 'bout some clothes? a shower?" We ignored him.

23 I went and got clothes from the freebox and washed off my new skin.

The rest of the nomads packed up and left so I found a ride to Gilman. Late that night Tim came into the show and told

me the cops were still
in front of the University
dressed in Riot gear in
that stiff position they
use. They'd been there for
hours waiting for the end
of the world to attack them.

Write to SP@M at:

WWC 5887
PO BOX 9000
ASHEVILLE NC
28815-9000

STEAL THIS RADIO

EVERY FRIDAY NIGHT!

88.7 FM

LOWER EAST SIDE

EXTENDED REMIX THANKYOU LIST FOR SHELTER, FOOD, SUPPORT, AND INSPIRATION:
BLACKOUT BOOKS, ABC-NO-RIO, BULLET SPACE, SCUMWRENCHES(RIP?...NAH!),
JIM FLEMMING AND THE AUTONOMEDIA CREW, KEITH AND STEPHANIE (BOOKMOBILE/
CIRCUS POSSE), DOS BLANCOS, A SPACE PHILI, KILLTIME, STALAG 13, NOTSQUAT,
BEN FLETCHER COMM. CENTER, MEGAN AND BUTTHOOK MANOR, STAYFREE SQUAT (RIP),
WOODEN SHOE BOOKS, MOTH AND TANDI, CIRCUS APOCALYPSE, PITTSBURG FNB'S,
JEFF PIPER AND THE DAYTON CLAN, JILL AND CESILIE AND CO., TANYA, SEAN, SUPA,
KIM, IGNATZ, ZIMO, AND THE EXTENDED NATABARI FAMILY, RICK AND EVERYONE AT
THE COMPOUND, ATLANTA FNB's, LUANA AND ZACK, NEW YORK JOHNNY, BALAAM, LIZ,
DAVE, THE WHOLE PHUCKHARWEE CLAN AND EVERYONE WHO HELPED SET UP THE AUSTIN
SHINDIG, MATTY, ATOM, THE WHOLE CLARKE ST. CREW AND EVERYONE WHO WORKED ON
THE BOF GATHERING, EAST BAY FNB'S, BERKELEY FREE RADIO, LONG HAUL, GILMAN
ST., SURVIVAL RESEARCH LAB., ICKY'S TEA HOUSE, HILLCREST HOUSE, EUGENE FNB'S,
POWERHAUS, PORTLAND FNB'S, SISTERS OF THE ROAD, SCOTTY's FOLKS, LA QUENA,
REJOICE AND EVERYONE WHO PUT ENERGY INTO THE VANCOUVER GATHERING, THE BLUE
LADY, DERRICK, PHOENIX AND THAT CREW, ARON, STEVE RIFE, THAT CHURCH WHERE
ALL THE PUNKS GO TO EAT IN MPLS, RAINBOW FOODS, A ZONE CHICAGO, THE PHARMACY,
THE QUESTION MARK IN THE SKY POSSE OF TEW, DREAMTIME VILLAGE, RICK AND HIS
VAN, SPECIAL THANKS TO EVERYONE WHO SENT ME STUFF AFTER THE FACT, CHRIS FLASH
FOR THE SLICK V-LOX CONNECTION, PHOTO FOLKS: SUPA, KATHY, MARTINE, RHEA, ARON,
THE MYSTERY LADY WHO LENT ME HER COMPUTER FOR THREE MONTHS, GAIL FURMAN, KC,
JANE AND CHRIS WHO I LOVE, ERIC D., OF COURSE THANKS TO FLY, STEFANE, ARROW,
DAVE, AND MY AMAZING MOM FOR SHELTER IN THE LAST FEW MONTHS, THE FIFTY
MILLION FUCKING OTHER PEOPLE THAT AREN'T ON THIS LIST AND SHOULD BE INCLUDING
YOU PROBABLY, EVERYONE WHO TRAVELED WITH US LAST SUMMER, AND EVERYONE OUT
THERE STRUGGLING FOR AUTONOMY AND FREEDOM FROM OPRESSION IN ANY WAY SHAPE OR
FORM - THIS IS FOR YOU. MY SOUL IN A JAR FOR A GLANCE IN MY DIRECTION FROM
SCOTT BEIBIN- MY EDITOR/CO-CONSPIRITOR GUY.

GRAFIX CREDITS:
COVER BY STACIE JASCOT (CHAOS GRAFIK BY SEAN LEE)
CREATE THE WEB/INDEP. SURVIVAL SYSTEMS -STACIE J.
TRUST YOUR DESIRES - I WISH I KNEW..
SURVIVAL -ONE OF A PACK OF ZIA TAROT CARDS BY STEPHAN
JAMBA - THE DUMPSTER GODDESS/GOD - JILL BURGESS
SEVENTH STREET SQUAT PHOTO COLLAGE
THE TANK - ERIC DROOKER
SQUATTERS RIGHTS GRAFIK - SABRINA JONES
RIOT - SETH TOBOCMAN
SMASHED TV'S AND FLOWERS - ERIC (MPLS.)
NOMFEST PHILADELPHIA FLYER - STACIE J. AND ARROW
MAXIMIZE POTENTIAL FOR EMERGENCE - STACIE J.
DROPOUT CIRCUS - COMING TO YOUR TOWN - JILL B.
CULT OF DOMESTICITY - DENNIS LUNDBERG
CONTAGIOUS MAGIC FLYER - SEAN LEE
LITTLE FIVE POINTS PARADE FLYER - ZIMO?
LET'S EAT! FLYER - TANYA ARANDA
OK DAD FESTIVAL COMIC - STEVE RIFE
NOMAD CIRCUS FLYER - NIMBY PHUCKHARWEE
801 G. BACKROUND - ANGLE WITH GAS MASK - NIMBY
GRAFIX FROM PATCH STORY - ALL A MYSTERY
CORVUS CORAX FLYER - (DIRTBAG) MIKE AND REN?
MONEY HIGHWAY - ANOTHER ONE OF THOSE MYSTERIES
BORN OF FIRE GRAFIK - (EAST BAY) ATOM
ICKY'S TEA HOUSE FLYER - ROOT MUGWART
WE ARE ONE! BACKROUND GRAFIX - AMY S. AND ARON
VANCOUVER ANARCHIST FLYER - POSSIBLY MARTHA?
HIGHLINE JOURNEY GRAFIK - AMY SCHIMPF
TWIN CITIES NOMFEST STUFF - STEVE RIFE
ALL DAT GRAFIX AND PUPPETS - ARON
THINKING WICKED THOUGHTS STENCIL - KATHY SANDOVAL

PHOTO CREDITS: SUPA GROVER, KATHY S., MARTINE, REAH, ARON.

ALL THE LAYOUT WAS TRIAL + ERROR + I FUCKED UP A LOT - BUT I GOT ADVICE ALONG THE WAY FROM (THE MASTERS) - SCOTT BEIBIN. AARON E., CINDY O., JIM FLEMMING, + FLY AMONG MANY OTHERS

THANK TO CHRIS FLASH FOR THE SLICK VELOX HOOK-UP

THANKS TO FOLKS FOR SHELTER ALONG THE WAY: FLY, STEFANE, ARROW, DAVE.

AND OF COURSE MY WONDERFUL MOM WHO HAS PUT UP WITH MY DEADBEAT SELF FOR A LITTLE TOO LONG..

LAST LINE ON PAGE #15 IS TAKEN FROM A SONG BY ERIC D. WHO IS A TOTAL INSPIRATION TO ME

GRAFIK ON PAGE 114 CARE OF THE DISAPPEARING - BRIAN KOZ

THANKS TO EVERYONE WHO LET ME USE THER COMPUTERS + VARIOUS PRINTING STUFF - ESPECIALLY STONE + CHRIS WHO I KEPT UP TILL 3:00 AM THE OTHER MORNING

This is the first in a series
of publications about living
life and surviving in a dying
world. Please pass this book
on to a friend. The next one
will be called RETRIEVAL INC!
It's all about scams vs. the
corporations and governments
that seek to oppress all people.
If you want to stay in touch or
stick in your 2 cents write me
at Bloodlink. hearts&farts Scott

THIS ZINE IS DEDICATED TO FELIX.

STEFANE + ARROW'S BABY GIRL - BORN NOVEMBER 6th, 1995

MORE TITLES FROM AUTONOMEDIA/SEMIOTEXT(E)

MILLENNIUM   Hakim Bey

T.A.Z.   The Temporary Autonomous Zone, Ontological Anarchy, Poetic Terrorism   Hakim Bey

SHOWER OF STARS   The Dream & The Book   Peter Lamborn Wilson

BLOOD AND VOLTS   Edison, Tesla & The Electric Chair   Th. Metzger

DREAMER OF THE DAY   Francis Parker Yockey & The Secret NAzi International   Kevin Coogan

BEYOND BOOKCHIN   Toawrd a Future Social Ecology   David Watson

SOUNDING OFF!   Music as SUbversion, Resistance, Revolution   Ron Sakolskly & Fred Wei-han Ho, eds.

THIS IS YOUR FINAL WARNING!   Thom Metzger

CASSETTE MYTHOS   The New Music Underground   Robin James, ed.

FRIENDLY FIRE   Bob Black

THE DAUGHTER   Roberta Allen

THE LIZARD CLUB   Steve Abbott

MAGPIE REVERIES   The Iconographic Mandalas of James Koehnline

FIRST & LAST EMPERORS   The Absolute State & the Body of the Despot   Kenneth Dean & Brian Massumi

INVISIBLE GOVERNANCE   The Art of African Micropolitics   David Hecht & Maliqalim Simone

ON ANARCHY & SCHIZOANALYSIS   Rolando Perez

GOD & PLASTIC SURGERY   Marx, Nietzsche, Freud & The Obvious   Jeremy Barris

MARX BEYOND MARX   Lessons on the Grundrisse   Antonio Negri

THE NARRATIVE BODY   Eldon Garnet

MODEL CHILDREN   Inside the Republic of Red Scarves   Paul Thorez

ABOUT FACE   Race in Postmodern America   Maliqalim Simone

COLUMBUS & OTHER CANNIBALS   The Wétiko Disease & the White Man   Jack Forbes

METATRON   Sol Yurick

SCANDAL   Essays in Islamic Heresy   Peter Lamborn Wilson

CLIPPED COINS   John Locke's Philosophy of Money   Constantine G. Caffentzis

HORSEXE   Essay on Transsexuality   Catherine Millot

THE TOUCH   Michael Brownstein

ARCANE OF REPRODUCTION   Housework, Prostitution, Labor & Capital   Leopoldina Fortunati

TROTSKYISM & MAOISM   A. Belden Fields

FILM & POLITICS IN THE THIRD WORLD   John Downing, ed.

ENRAGÉS & SITUATIONISTS IN THE OCCUPATION MOVEMENT   René Viénet

ZEROWORK   the Anti-Work Anthology   Bob Black & Tad Kepley, eds.

MIDNIGHT OIL   Work, Energy, War, 1973 – 1992   Midnight Notes Collective

PURE WAR   Paul Virilio & Sylvère Lotringer

WALKING THROUGH CLEAR WATER IN A POOL PAINTED BLACK   Cookie Mueller

STILL BLACK, STILL STRONG   Dhoruba bin Wahad, Mumia Abu-Jamal, Assata Shakur

HANNIBAL LECTER, MY FATHER   Kathy Acker

METATRON   Sol Yurick

HOW I BECAME ONE OF THE INVISIBLE   David Rattray

GONE TO CROATAN   Origins of North American Dropout Culture   Ron Saklolsky & James Koehnline, eds.

SEMIOTEXT(E) ARCHITECTURE   Hraztan Zeitlian, ed.

SEMIOTEXT(E) USA   Jim Fleming & Peter Lamborn Wilson, eds.

OASIS   Maliqalim Simone, et al., eds.

POLYSEXUALITY   François Peraldi, ed.

THE ARCHEOLOGY OF VIOLENCE   Pierre Clastres

FATAL STRATEGIES   Jean Baudrillard

For every little piece of history that was ever crammed down your throat back when you were in primary school, for every washed-over tale of conquest and domination, textbook stories of victorious battles, heroes, villains, martyrs and for every tale about discovered lands and empires rising out of the sites of wars, there was always the other stories you never heard. The stories of genocide and colonization, annihilated cultures and wiped out civilizations, underground movements and small patches of subculture thriving beneath the surface of monolithic dominions.

With the ever-increasing corporate media stranglehold rapidly encroaching in our society and our large scale venues of expression quickly becoming incorporated into huge octopus-like conglomerates owned by people who care of nothing but increasing and propagating their ideas of division and hate, it grimly leads us to wonder what sort of (if any) glossed-over soulless fashionshow picture will be painted for our future generations about any real youth subculture movements in the 1990s. Whoever controls the present always controls the past, and with all of our little voices drowning in a sea of soulless vapid trashy fucking garbage being spewed forth like white noise to drown out any meager words of protest as the tanks come rolling through, most people don't even know we exist in the present day.

What you hold in your hands is a piece of our history. It's a collection of stories from all over the country, woven together in the squatter community in New York City, telling the tale of what a bunch of young people did with the Summer back at the end of the 20th Century in North America. Originally published as a scam xeroxed zine and distributed amongst ourselves through the scattered nomadic traveling network some of us call home, a few of these copies will hopefully reach a larger audience and maybe plant a few seeds of inspiration in minds not as familiar with the stuff we do and the lives we lead. You don't have to look too closely to see that it's more than a story about a few friends getting together to explore in the cities across the highways and freight-train lines of this country. It's a document about a world we're building out of the wastes of this self-destructing modern consumer industrial society we've found ourselves living in the middle of; a life we're creating for ourselves outside the reach of the law in a country whose sheltered ruling elite is growing fat off the profits of the new jail industry and prison labor force and thriving off of the fear instilled in the general population by our paranoid TV cop culture.

(Continued on back cover)